DEAR
DAUGHTER
OF A
NARCISSISTIC
MOTHER ...

DEAR DAUGHTER OF A NARCISSISTIC MOTHER ...

DANU MORRIGAN

DARTON·LONGMAN+TODD

First published in 2017 by
Darton, Longman and Todd Ltd
1 Spencer Court
140 – 142 Wandsworth High Street
London SW18 4JJ

Reprinted 2018

ISBN: 978-0-232-53277-7

Produced by Judy Linard
Printed and bound in Great Britain by Bell & Bain, Glasgow

Contents

Contents

DEAR
DAUGHTER
OF A
NARCISSISTIC
MOTHER ...

Dear fellow daughter of a narcissistic mother ...

For the past two years I have sent a weekly email letter to thousands of women who, like you, are the daughter of a narcissistic mother. These letters aim to *support, encourage, inform and validate* these women, and the regular feedback I get shows the value they get (see some of the feedback below).

This book is the compilation of those letters, a full 100 letters in all, and I hope and intend this book will likewise support, encourage, inform and validate you too.

Although these letters expand on the information on my website www.daughtersofnarcissisticmothers.com, and in my book *You're Not Crazy – It's Your Mother*, they do stand alone. So if this is the first of my work you've read, you will still get full value from it.

You can get these letters for free by signing up to the *Guidebook to Healing and Thriving* on the website, but as they are sent weekly it will take you a full two years to get them all, instead of having all this valuable information right now, in one place, to hold in your hand and keep.

My hope and intention is that these letters will be your route-map, guide and even friend on your journey to full healing from your toxic upbringing, and thriving in your life going forward.

Here is a sample of the value other daughters of narcissistic mothers have got from these letters:

'The letters are coming out in a book? That's great!!!!! I would like to have the letters to read over for meditation. I learn something every time I go back and reread them.' Anonymous by request

'Your site and your weekly letters have been not only empowering, but incredibly vindicating. I won't say I couldn't have done it without them, but they certainly helped conceive my rebirth and encourage it to grow and flourish.' CHS, Santa Ana

'I find your descriptions of specific details and emotional landscape are really enlightening and validating for the type of emotions and experiences I encounter, which I may not be realizing myself, because

of the usual mental unclarity, confusion, fog and such things. You put names and words and meaning to these experiences, and that is so useful, like a breeze of air in a stuffed room.' Alevtina, Kiev, Ukraine

'Your letters have been a godsend. I can't tell you how much they have helped me.' S.D.

✳

So, who am I, and why would you listen to me?

I am a fellow daughter of narcissistic mother (DONM as we refer to it for shorthand). I have no professional qualifications in anything to do with this topic, so I do not talk down to you from any academic pedestal. Instead, I come to you from the trenches of the lived experience. I'm still on this journey, and I have lots to learn and many roads to take yet. But I have corresponded with thousands of DONMs over the last 8 years, and ran a forum for four of those, during which I learned so much about the DONM experience. This hard-earned information is what I share with you.

Also, as a professional writer anyway, my job is to present information in a way that makes sense, and that's what I offer. Many many DONMs tell me that I explain their experiences – their confusing, bewildering, hard-to-understand experiences – in a way that makes sense to them for the first time. As more than one DONM has told me, 'You explain my life to me in a way I never could.'

I hope and trust I can do the same for you in the following letters.

Hugs,

Danu

Introduction ...

I truly believe that healing and thriving is possible for those of us who were unfortunate enough to be raised by a mother with Narcissistic Personality Disorder. We are not on an easy journey for sure, and it's unfair that we have to work so hard to just get to a place where other women – those who had loving mothers – started. But that's the way it is, and we deserve to have all the resources we need to help us as we travel.

I invite you to consider, acknowledge, applaud and even celebrate your sheer courage. Most people never can bring themselves to examine whether their relationship with their mother is toxic. That you have done so is a huge step and truly I do hope you're so proud of yourself for having done that.

Until you acknowledged the toxicity of the way your mother raised you, and still treats you, no change was possible. Now that you have acknowledged this huge truth, all things become possible.

Having said that, if you're like many DONMs you might be still struggling to really accept that she was, indeed, toxic. It's not surprising, is it, given that she probably spent years telling you that *she* was perfect and everything was all your fault, that you were over-reacting, or over-sensitive?

I'm still on this journey myself, but I have been on it for a good number of years, many of them before I knew about Narcissistic Personality Disorder.

At that time I thought I was fixing a flawed me, rather than healing an injured me. And of course the same is true for you: You are injured and requiring healing, rather than flawed and requiring fixing as she told you.

Now, what I share here are my own opinions and perceptions and understandings. They are based on those years of searching and learning and communication with thousands of DONMs, and are my best shot at figuring it all out. But please please *judge everything I say on its own merits, not because I said it.*

I am only a fellow-traveller, and I share my thoughts, but they're not holy writ or anything like it.

But having said that, don't automatically dismiss what I say either. Sometimes what you believe and *'know'* isn't true. It's the residue of your narcissistic mother's brainwashing. And those false beliefs can lead you to dismiss anything contrary to that brainwashing. Indeed, often the more important it is for you to hear something, the more vehemently your existing beliefs will make you dismiss it.

But here's the thing: You need a new way of thinking and of being in the world, as part of your *'freeDONM'*. The old way is your mother's way, and that's not working for you or you wouldn't be seeking answers. So don't automatically dismiss what I write. I didn't pull it out of nowhere; a lot of thought and learning and thinking and exploring went into all that I say, and there may well be value in it for you. But, neither should you uncritically accept it. I do my very best to share good information and accurate perceptions, but I could be wrong about any or all of it. So, be open-minded and don't automatically reject what I write, but don't automatically accept it either. Judge it on its own merits as I said.

One major tool I'll be referring to again and again is Emotional Freedom Technique (EFT). EFT has literally changed my life for the better, and I am so excited to share it with you. It is a process of tapping on acupuncture points to release, erase and evaporate negative emotions and limiting beliefs. This has huge benefits for us, as you'll see. I invite you to visit my website at http://www.daughtersofnarcissisticmothers.com/emotional-freedom-technique/ to learn more about it and get the free instructions there.

In each letter I speak of different issues DONMs face and for many of them I recommend EFT, as so many of our challenges are caused by our limiting emotions and beliefs.

Having said that, I want you to get value out of these letters even if you decide not to even try EFT, so I do my best to offer other alternatives too. In each case the alternative would be, in my opinion, slower and clumsier than EFT, simply because

EFT is so quick and efficient, but I do want to give you the choice.

I am honoured that you are walking this part of the journey with me, and hope and trust that it will be a good one.

Hugs,

Danu

Are you a bird trapped against a window?

Dear DONM ...

You know that famous phrase about the definition of madness? It's to keep on doing the same things but expecting a different result.

And we DONMs do that with our mothers. We keep going to her hoping that *this* time it'll be different. *This time* she'll be the mother we need her to be. *This time* she'll surely support us in our grief, applaud us in our success, accept us for who we are with no agenda.

And she never does.

When I think of this dynamic (which I, too, did for far too many years) I think of a bird flying fruitlessly into a window, again and again.

It breaks my heart. It breaks my heart for me, and for all of us.

I do understand this pattern, and I do forgive myself for doing it, as I hope you can forgive yourself.

It's totally natural to want our mothers to love us, so no wonder we keep trying. Especially since we believed her constant message that *she* was perfect and *we* were the ones so flawed that it caused all the problems – so it made sense that we were the ones who held the solution to fixing the dysfunctional relationship.

But, that was a lie, wasn't it? A big fat total nasty lie.

The problem in the relationship lies in no flaw in us, but in the fact that she has Narcissistic Personality Disorder. The fact is that narcissists *cannot* change and *will not* change and cannot even see that there is anything *to* change.

You might know that rationally, but not know it deep down, where it counts, where you need to know it.

However, the sooner we realise this truth – really, deep down, at the core of us – the sooner we are truly free.

Once you accept that truth, you are free to make healthy

decisions about your life, and we'll be exploring many of those options later.

You'll free up more energy than you ever thought possible ... all that energy that is currently wasted flying into that window will be freed up for you to use for your healing and then for your thriving.

That freedom is priceless, and it is only a decision away.

Okay, making that decision is not easy. Try journaling about it, or using affirmations, or maybe discuss it with your therapist. Or use EFT. EFT is perfect for taking what you know rationally, and making it a core deep-down belief. You end up *feeling* it's true in all of your body, as well as just knowing it's true in your head.

When you let go of the useless hope that your narcissistic mother will change, you free yourself from constantly flying into that window. You stop trying to do the impossible, and that will give you time and energy to start creating the possible: in other words, *your own life, lived your way*.

I fervently have that wish for you, and for all of us DONMs.

Hugs,

Danu

Surfing your anger

Dear DONM …

Note: As we are discussing how to experience and process anger, I share tools such as EFT/Tapping which I fully believe are safe, but you need to know you are totally accepting responsibility for your use of, and experience with, these tools.

So: Often when you finally acknowledge and accept the abuse that was done to you, you can experience anger. Rage even. Fury like you have never known before, to a depth you didn't realise you could manifest.

This rage will probably take you by surprise, and may feel overwhelming and intimidating. You probably are not used to it as you, no doubt, were not allowed to express any anger.

What's happening is that your mother-imposed filters have been removed and you are now seeing clearly for the first time and you realise that – hell yes! – what she did to you was wrong. Beyond wrong, even. And all that suppressed anger is coming up to be experienced.

And this is good news! I know it feels scary and perhaps even out of control, and overwhelming as I said. But bear with it. I'll give you ideas in a minute on how to process it. But for now, just bear with the anger … just let it be … just allow it. It won't overwhelm you no matter how it feels like it might.

This anger is righteous anger. You have every right to be angry at the injustices and abuse that were heaped upon you.

Along with this anger might come fantasies and/or dreams of doing her (them?) violence.

It shocked me when it happened to me. Here I was (am!) a pacifist, a genuine kind gentle soul, and yet I was having the most incredibly graphic and detailed visions of the violence I could do to both my parents.

I've thought a lot about this, and this is what I've come up with: I think those fantasies and dreams are okay. Maybe they're even necessary for healing.

When we were children we were powerless against our

abusers, but these fantasies allow us to reclaim our power. And the subconscious mind does not distinguish between reality and fantasy, so as far as it's concerned, you *have* reclaimed your power by doing this.

Now, needless to say, it is not right to act out these fantasies. No one is advocating that you visit actual violence on your parents, or on anyone. That would be wrong on so many levels. It would be legally and morally wrong of course. But also wrong for you. Your healing does not consist of you sinking to their level. I so believe that it's true that the best revenge is living well, and you becoming a violent person is not living well. Doing actual violence would trap you in their dysfunction.

So don't do it.

But if your brain is bringing up fantasies or dreams, go with them, I suggest. In every case I have heard of, when other DONMs went through this, those thoughts passed in time, with no effort. It seemed to be a process that had to be gone through on the path to healing, is all.

I think the violent thoughts bring the narcissists down to size in our heads. It certainly did in mine. Before that, they loomed big and scary, as they did when I was a child. They had power over me. Now that I 'know' I can physically beat them, they seem small and scared. Pathetic even. They have no power over me, any more and that is so freeing.

The thing that sometimes we don't realise about anger is that it's our friend. It's a voice tugging on our sleeve saying, 'Er, somebody is mistreating you now.' The problem is when we cannot heed that voice. The anger then gets suppressed, and gets carried around with us until it's released. I do suspect that this repressed anger carries a huge burden. At the very least it takes a lot of energy to keep it pushed down – energy which could be used for other things from dancing to building a life.

And so, it is absolutely right and appropriate that this anger be felt, and experienced, and expressed and processed. And as part of that processing, it moves on. It needs to move on to be healthy. Anger that you are dwelling in, or swimming in, is just as unhealthy as anger that is repressed (arguably more so, indeed).

So what can you do to process it and move it on?

Just go with it. Accept it and enjoy the ride. Try to embrace it if you can – think of it like you're surfing the biggest baddest wave you can and it's equal parts fear and exhilaration. In the act of feeling it and experiencing it and acknowledging it, you are processing it.

Try to find the power in the anger. Only powerful people can afford to get angry, so this isn't a trick, it's real.

Know that it'll take the time it takes. I know that I said not to dwell or swim in the anger and that's true. But there is a lifetime of anger there, and so it'll take as long as it takes to process it.

There are ways of speeding it up though:

Maybe write out your anger – do freewriting perhaps – I share more about this in the next letter.

Use EFT. Just tap the points over and over while you are experiencing the anger. It might not feel like anything is happening, but it is working to process and move on that 'chapter' of the anger.

Even better, speak aloud as you tap. Speak whatever comes into your mind. Be as violent and aggressive as you need. Tap each statement on one point and move onto the next. For example: 'I hate her – I HATE what she did to me – She's a ******* bitch – How DARE she do that to me? – Oh God it hurts what she did to me – I'd like to kill her now.'

And even better still, walk while you're doing this. Just pace the room. There is something so empowering and healing about the kinaesthetic feeling of moving while you do the tapping and the speaking aloud. You can also tap and walk but not speak aloud, if that's not appropriate. The most powerful, however, is to do all three.

After a while – half an hour maybe; perhaps an hour, you will feel the anger disperse and you will have a kind of exhausted peace. That 'chapter' of anger is gone now, never to return. There will be more, until it's all gone, but you've done good work here.

Hugs,

Danu

Another free, wonderful, tool for healing

Dear DONM …

I wanted to talk to you today about freewriting.

Freewriting is just what it says – writing freely. It is a terrific tool for all sorts of purposes: for getting in touch with your subconscious to know what's really going on for you, for accessing buried emotions and processing them and moving on from them, and for increasing creativity.

What you do with freewriting is this: you put pen to paper and you write, without stopping, for a set length of time or a set number of pages. It is important that you put pen to paper rather than use the computer as freewriting is a very kinaesthetic process, it's about being *in* your body and using your body, and physical handwriting facilitates that much more than typing on a computer. I do recommend a pen rather than pencil for ease of writing quickly, and I have even experimented with different pens to find the smoothest ones.

When you start this, your hand can get tired, but just persevere and your hand will get stronger soon.

The most important aspect to freewriting is this: write quickly, without stopping, and do not worry about the quality. It does not matter *what* you write, only that you *do* write. By freeing yourself from worrying about what you write, you switch off the internal critic and that is hugely freeing, especially for us DONMs who have been so accustomed to constant criticism.

When you freewrite, you are responsible for the quantity (the agreed time or pages amount), but bear no responsibility for the quality. Do not fret over the words you use, or your spelling, or your grammar, or the quality of your handwriting. Your success comes from doing it, not from how it is done.

There are various ways you can incorporate freewriting in your life. One of the most famous is what's called Morning Pages (made famous by Julia Cameron in her excellent book

The Artist's Way). You keep a notebook and pen beside your bed, and as soon as you wake up in the morning, while your mind is still half-asleep, before your inner critic has time to wake up, you write three pages. (You can go to the toilet first if you need to, of course! But apart from that, the ideal is to do this before you get up, or have coffee, or any other morning routines).

The three pages should be fairly big – A4 in Europe and the equivalent in America. This is important as I will explain in a minute.

So, what do you write? Anything. Again, don't judge it. I often start off with a comment on the weather that I see through the window. I write about how I feel, physically – still tired, or refreshed, any aches I have, etc. I might write about what happened yesterday, or my hopes for today. A lot of it, frankly, is hugely banal stuff, but *that's okay*!

The essential thing is to keep the hand moving. In a way, if you commit to keeping the pen moving, the writing happens *through* you and not *by* you. The words come, and if they don't, just write that fact, like this: 'I don't know what to write next, not sure what to say now, no idea what to write …'

If I filled three pages with that, it would still be good because I would still have done the exercise. But, in practice what happens is that the brain gets bored with writing like that, and after two or three lines I'll find I'm writing something more solid. When I say 'I find I'm writing', that's exactly what it's like. I don't think what to write and then write it. I write and see what comes flowing out of the pen.

I can tend to be somewhat ADD, and doing three pages in one go was tough at the start. But that was okay – I just wrote my frustration at it: 'God I resent doing this. I'm so bored now. This is ridiculous. Why am I doing this? I wonder what happened on my favourite sites overnight …' But even as I'm writing that, it means I'm still writing and so still doing it correctly.

Three pages is the magic number because that is long enough to let the top layer of crud out of your brain and begin to get into deeper layers underneath. This doesn't happen immediately – I have frequently written three pages of extremely banal drivel, with no insights coming at all. But if insights do come, they come on the third page.

I see patterns. I find I'm writing about the same topic over and over, revisiting it without realising why. But I therefore realise that this topic is obviously important to me.

I have dallied with freewriting many times before, but about six weeks ago I committed to it. And there have been huge shifts in my life since, for the better. Coincidence? Perhaps. I think not though.

And even without the shifts, even if they *were* coincidental, I am finding it hugely rewarding to do. The first thing is that I can guarantee myself to start every day with a success. That is so empowering and really does set me up for the day. And it does give me insights into what's going on for me. Among the banality and whinging there are gems of awareness which really do make sense to me and help me.

So I do recommend it hugely.

Other ways to use freewriting is if you have a problem or a decision to make, freewrite about that. Say you are debating taking a job or moving to another city or a big decision like that. You could set the timer for say 15 minutes and just start writing your thoughts about the dilemma.

Or write your pain and upset at an incident, either recent or in the past. In this way you're using freewriting to process your emotions and let them go. As we discussed before, emotions cannot hurt you, so do not be scared of this.

And, as a DONM, you can use freewriting to explore how you feel about all that happened to you. You can write a letter to a younger you, or a letter from a younger you. You can write to your narcissistic mother and say all you want to say. (Without sending it of course. This is for you.)

Freewriting is a hugely powerful tool and I do invite you to use it.

Hugs,

Danu

Your grief and bereavement

Dear DONM …

Once you have truly accepted that your narcissistic mother has never loved you, *can* never love you, and *will* never love you, a number of things will happen.

The first is that, as explained previously, you will finally be free of banging your head against the wall, of flying constantly into the window. Free of trying to achieve the impossible.

That is the good news.

However, there is a downside to it, in that you may well experience huge sadness and grief. This makes perfect sense when you think about it – you absolutely have suffered a huge loss, a massive bereavement.

You have, in a very real sense, lost your mother, just as much as if she had died. You are experiencing the death of the image of the loving, kind, decent, supportive mother you hoped and even believed she would one day become.

That is truly a loss which is not to be underestimated.

This grief is made worse, I believe, because it's such a private grief. In the case of a real death, society supports us in our grieving, and understands what we're going through, and our friends rally around, and there is a cultural framework in the form of a funeral to help us through this grief.

In the case of letting go of the hope our mother will ever change, there is no such help. Unless we're very lucky, even our spouses and close friends won't understand.

As for getting through the grief, just know that, as with all grief, time itself will help with that, at least to some extent.

Here are a few steps to help you process it though.

First, don't underestimate the enormity of what you're going through. Be gentle with yourself at this time. Understand that you might feel weepy and upset just as if you had experienced a literal bereavement. I do suggest you honour this and don't dismiss it, and above all don't beat yourself up for it.

If at all possible do enrol the help of friends and spouses/partners. They probably will not understand, but if they choose to, they can help even without understanding. If they simply take your word for it that this is, for you, like it would be for them if their loving mother died, then they can offer the same support they would like to have in that circumstance.

Freewriting will help you to work through the grief.

Another option to help with the grief is EFT. EFT is really good for processing emotions, and the emotion of grief is no different. You can just tap the points as you're feeling the sadness and grief.

The most important thing is to know that this grief will pass, it will ease, and that joy and peace are waiting for you.

Hugs,

Danu

The trauma you suffered

Dear DONM …

Could you be suffering from PTSD? Post-Traumatic Stress Disorder.

Nonsense, you might say. That's only for those who experienced a war zone, or other similar intense tragedy.

The thing is, in many ways, being raised in a narcissistic household is like being in a war zone. The constant stress and fear is very similar.

What you might have is Complex PTSD, or C-PTSD.

Wikipedia describes it like this:

'Complex post-traumatic stress disorder (C-PTSD) is a psychological injury that results from protracted exposure to prolonged social and/or interpersonal trauma in the context of either captivity or entrapment (i.e. the lack of a viable escape route for the victim) that results in the lack or loss of control, helplessness, and deformations of identity and sense of self.

Forms of trauma associated with C-PTSD include sexual abuse (especially child sexual abuse), physical abuse, emotional abuse, domestic violence or torture – all repeated traumas in which there is an actual or perceived inability for the victim to escape.'

Doesn't that sound exactly like our situation?

EFT is superb for clearing trauma. For actually erasing it. Either work with an EFT practitioner, or by yourself which is very doable. Or, if you don't wish to use EFT, do consider getting yourself good therapy to work with the trauma. Or both of course: EFT and therapy. EMDR is another excellent resource.

Don't underestimate what you experienced, and do claim all the resources you need to heal it, I suggest.

Hugs,

Danu

What about telling siblings?

Dear DONM …

There can be a big temptation, when you find out the truth about your mother's narcissism, to want to share it with siblings and others.

That's totally understandable. You feel that you are free now that you know the truth, or freer at least, and you want to help them be free too. They might even be allies with you in dealing with your mother. It'll be great!

But steady on.

This can be a tricky one to manoeuvre. It's a big step, and not one that is to be taken lightly. It can very easily backfire on you.

Your siblings may well have a very different relationship with your mother than you do. They might be the favourite child who can do no wrong (known as the Golden Child), while you are the one who can never do right (the scapegoat). Their relationship with her might be working well for them, albeit in a dysfunctional co-dependent way. They most likely will not want that disturbed.

Or, even if their relationship with her is fraught, they may not be ready to hear the truth. As you have possibly experienced yourself, it's hugely upsetting to learn that your own mother does not love you, that she cannot love you and will not love you ever. It demands a whole rethink of your life, your Self, everything. So, your sibling might not be in a place to hear it.

And so, not able to hear it, needing to defend themselves from this unwelcome news, they can react badly. Aggressively even. They perceive it as an attack – which it is, really – an attack on their current reality, no matter how helpfully you mean it or kindly you say it.

And so, as attacked people tend to do, they defend themselves in any way possible. They could turn on you, asking how dare you say such horrible nasty things about your lovely sainted mother. They may refuse to talk to you, cut off contact either temporarily or permanently.

They may even go back and tell your mother what you're saying about her – and the stuff will really hit the fan then.

So, that's it then? You've no choice but to leave them wallowing in the pain and dysfunction and abuse? You've escaped from it, but they have to keep enduring it?

That, of course, is the dilemma.

You do have a choice as to whether to tell them or not. And you have to make that choice.

And there is no right answer.

You know them best. They might be delighted to hear the news. It might feel like the key to the prison gates.

But, as described above, they might not. How do you know which it will be?

The trick, I think, is to start with small questions. If you're used to venting at each other about her, maybe say something like, 'Why do you think she's like this?' and see what they say, if they're up for exploring the topic.

Or if you've never spoken before about her behaviour, start with that: Does it annoy you when she does x?', and see how responsive your sibling is to discussing it. Watch out for signs of your sibling closing up or getting defensive, and back off immediately if that happens.

If they seem receptive, ask another small question, or make a small observation and see how that goes.

If your sibling isn't ready to hear this, then you need to respect that. It's horrible to see them still suffering when you know the answer, but truly you can't do anything about that. You can stay alert for signs that they might be shifting in their openness as time passes, and test them every so often on their willingness by using another small question.

Hugs,

Danu

Normal rules don't apply
with narcissists

Dear DONM …

One of the biggest weapons that narcissists use against us is our manners. They put us in no-win situations where our niceness and our decency and our social awareness work against us.

Classic example: We're not talking to them. We don't want to talk to them. We might even have gone No Contact (which means to formally sever all contact between them and us). We might even have informed them that we are No Contact and they are not to contact us.

But a gift arrives in the post for us, or for a member of our family. And of course it would be so rude to not acknowledge that, so we need to send a thank-you letter. And in this way we fall into her trap of contacting her again.

However – the good news is that no, we don't have to thank her!

We don't have to fall into any trap.

Here's the thing:

With narcissists, the normal rules don't apply. That might seem quite radical, but it's really good news. They break all the rules of social interaction and human co-operation, after all, and therefore we are not bound to those rules when we're dealing with them.

I repeat, they have broken the rules of society already. They consistently do this. And so you are at a serious disadvantage if you keep playing by those rules. Which is, of course, what they are counting on.

Can you imagine playing, say, golf, with somebody who wouldn't play by the rules? Instead of playing the ball as it lay, your opponent would pick it up each time and put it in a position favourable to herself, to allow for easy putting. Or maybe even just pick it up and drop it in the hole.

You, on the other hand, scrupulously keep to the rules. You are not going to start cheating when it's your turn.

This is partly because of the narcissist's web of confusion: the cheating is so subtle you don't notice it, or it's so blatant you can't believe it, and therefore discount it as something you imagined.

And the other reason you don't cheat is because you're a decent, kind person who wants to play by the rules.

Now, of you and her, who is going to win that golf game? And every future game? And by what huge margin?

The only recourse is to either stop playing (and we'll be talking about that soon), or to 'cheat' in your turn.

But 'cheat' is an emotive term, and my analogy falls down there. Because it's not cheating. It's recognising that what you're playing is not golf, no matter how much you thought it was golf, no matter how often she tells you it's golf, and no matter how much you want to keep to the rules of golf.

You're playing a different game, with different rules, and in many ways, no rules at all.

And so it's fine for you to break the rules of 'golf', when it's not golf you're playing.

I know it goes against the grain, and can seem shocking to do, but once you get the hang of it, it is very liberating.

So, you don't have to thank them for gifts (such gifts really just being drama-fodder and manipulation anyway and not genuine gifts).

You don't have to send them birthday cards or other cards.

You don't have to include them in your family celebrations. (I had both my 40th birthday party and a book launch without inviting my parents, and it was the best decision both times.)

You don't have to return their phone calls, texts, or emails.

You don't have to 'friend' them on Facebook, or respond to their statuses if they are a friend.

The only rule that you need to worry about is the rule to protect yourself and your family from her manipulation.

So I suggest you watch out for the times she tries to manipulate you into doing things because it's the polite thing to do ... and refuse to fall for it.

Normal rules don't apply with narcissists. That's half their power; they don't play by the rules while knowing we will. We regain our power by realising that, when it comes to dealing with them, the rules don't apply to us either.

Hugs,

Danu

Introducing Rule 1

Dear DONM …

One of the things I noticed again and again when I was running the forum was that women would often ask us what they should do in a specific circumstance. It really wasn't our place to tell them what to do, but I totally understood why they were asking: their narcissistic mothers had them so confused that half the time they didn't realise what they *could* do, what they *should* do, what they were *allowed* to do, and so on.

And so we introduced a rule called Rule 1. This rule is: *Do what you want to do*. (Of course, we also had Rule 2, which was: *If in doubt refer to Rule 1*.)

It was often somewhat mind-blowing for these women to be told this amazing concept. Not surprisingly, it never occurred to them before that they could do what they wanted to do when their narcissistic mother had spent a lifetime telling them they had to do what *she* wanted them to do.

We DONMs were taught so much, so hard, so long, and so convincingly, that our needs, wants, and desires did not matter at all, that it is very difficult for us to realise that they *do* matter.

Our needs, wants and desires matter hugely.

This can be a whole new mind-set.

The first thing to accept is the very concept itself: that it's okay to want your own way sometimes. To know that sometimes it *is* about you, and *what is important is what you want*, rather than what anyone else wants.

So, let that sink in for a moment, I suggest.

Think about it.

Does it feel scary? Does it feel enormous and threatening?

The very idea that it should be about what you want can seem very scary indeed when you are not used to that.

But, in your new life of freedom, or as we called it, *freeDONM*, this is essential to learn: *It is important that you do what you want to do*.

Now, of course we're not talking about being inappropriately selfish, or self-centred, or neglecting your responsibilities, or anything like that. If you have children, then for sure it is essential to meet their needs before your own desires. (Indeed meeting your own desires before your children's needs is a quintessentially narcissistic thing to do.)

Likewise, if you have a job, or a business, or other responsibilities, then of course you have to see to those and honour those.

But outside that kind of responsibility, truly, what *you* want is important and should be given a very high priority when you're making decisions about what you're going to do or not do.

And so, the answer to any dilemma you might have is: *Do what you want to do*.

So, if it is your birthday and your mother wants you to spend it with her but you were dreading the idea, then you need only ask yourself, 'What do *I* want to do?'

If you were dreading spending the day with her, then it is very clear that you do not want to do this. So by Rule 1, which is to do what *you* want to do, you do not spend the day with her. Instead you choose to spend your birthday in a way that supports you and is enjoyable for you.

Will there be repercussions? Yes, of course there will be. She will not be happy about this at all. She will even complain, or undergo narcissistic rage (which is like a temper tantrum for narcissists).

We'll discuss soon how to deal with her narcissistic rage. For now just start thinking about what you would like to do. Even if you're not in a position to actually do it yet, it's good to get the practice in even identifying what you want to do.

As ever, you can use EFT to help you identify this if you're not sure about it. Just tap using the phrase: *Even though I don't even know what I want to do, I love and accept myself anyway*, and use the rest of the process after that. In a very short time your actual real desires will bubble up and you will be very clear about what you want to do.

Hugs,

Danu

Dealing with the shame

Dear DONM …

The writer John Bradshaw called it Toxic Shame. It's not normal healthy shame that comes when we do something wrong, and which helps us behave well.

Rather, toxic shame is the shame we carry to our very core about who we are. And it's not surprising that DONMs have a lot of that. We were taught to be deeply ashamed of ourselves. We were taught that we were flawed, shameful, born broken. We had to be seen to be so damaged so she could be seen (by herself at least, but also by others) to be so perfect.

And we took that and carried it, because we knew no better. And we carry it still.

Feeling, like I said, that we are innately broken and damaged and grotesque. That if others knew this truth about us they'd never want anything to do with us. And so, always hiding ourselves, portraying what feels like a false self. And so feeling (and in one way, being) inauthentic as we hide what we think is our true selves.

The irony, of course, is that we are not the shameful twisted distorted self she told us we were, and that therefore the 'false self' we show the world is nearer to our real 'self' than the 'self' we think we are. Does that make sense?

I mean that we think we are hiding a non-existent nasty self, and portraying a nice real self, and we are the only one who doesn't realise. Our friends and family see the real true nice self. But we twist ourselves in knots hiding this big shameful secret, when there is no secret to hide at all.

Who we are is an ordinary, nice, decent, averagely-flawed human.

Now, to digress a bit, of course the 'self' we show is false to an extent.

As the poet T. S. Eliot put it, we put on a face to meet the faces that we meet. But I don't think it's false as such. We put on clothes to meet all but our closest intimates, and we put on metaphorical clothes for different situations.

But that just means that there are different roles for different relationships, different levels of exposure. The face we show to the world is just a dressed, polished, expression of ourselves. It's still us, just as a dressed us is still us.

So, that digression was to show that the public face we have is no lie, just a clothed version of the real self.

And, so, to get back to my main point, when we think of shame, is it possible to just know that we do not have to be ashamed? That we are okay just as we are. That our narcissistic mother's lies were layered onto us, wrapped around us, trying to force us into the shape of a gargoyle.

We can reject that. We can hand back that false shame.

One way is by recognising the shame when we feel it, and proactively giving ourselves a different message.

That might not be easy though as the shame is so subtle, so insidious. It flashes through our awareness quicker than we can tell, leaving just its scar.

But with practice and diligence it can be possible.

I, of course, suggest that Tapping/EFT is the way to deal with the shame the easy way, so I do invite you to try that.

Hugs,

Danu

Boundaries are
your greatest gift to yourself

Dear DONM …

I spoke of boundaries in *You're Not Crazy*, but they're so important I want to go into more detail about them here.

You are entitled to set your boundaries where you please, no matter if others think they're unreasonable. Indeed, you're entitled to them, no matter if they *are* unreasonable, to exaggerate for emphasis. If you said, for example, that people could only phone you between the hours of 2.00 and 2.30 each day, that's your right. Of course others have the right to find that boundary unreasonable, and to not call you at all. But they don't have the right to call at other times when you've stated it's not acceptable.

How much more does that truth apply if you are setting reasonable boundaries?

Boundaries are your birthright, and you are entitled to have them. And setting boundaries is telling the world – and more importantly, telling yourself – that you have value. That you are not their chew-toy. That you claim your own space, both literal and metaphorical.

I offer you the possibility of creating your own personal manifesto regarding your boundaries. Think about them, write them down. Writing things down has impact and power far beyond merely thinking of something.

It can be hard for DONMs to even think what their boundaries might be, as we have been so trained to not even consider our own boundaries, or even the possibility of having them. One suggestion is to think of what annoys you when it happens: that's a clue that one of your boundaries is being breached. So for example, if it really annoys you when your friend talks at you on the phone for hours, then a reasonable and legitimate boundary might be that you will not speak on the phone for more than half an hour. Or that she has to check before she starts whether it's a good time for you, and accept it gracefully if it's not.

Here is a list of possible boundaries – a menu for you from which to pick and choose, but please be clear that this is just to spark your imagination so you can think of your own.

- No one is allowed to just drop around to my house without phoning first.
- No one is allowed to let themselves into my house.
- Once in my house, no one is allowed to root around in the cupboards.
- No one is allowed to touch me without my permission.
- No one is allowed to comment adversely on my weight/ appearance/state of my house.
- I have the right to say, 'I'll think about it and get back to you', rather than being pressured into things.
- I have the right to change my mind.
- I have the right to say 'No' without further explanation.
- I have the right to not answer the phone if it does not suit me.
- I have the right to refuse to answer personal questions.
- I have the right to put limits on visits: 'You may call between 2.00 and 4.00'.

Now, of course sometimes you relax those boundaries. Spouses and children are allowed to touch you, for example. They're still keeping to the boundary though, as they already have permission. And I know that with my close friends, I'm quite entitled to go to the kitchen to make tea myself, as they are in my house. But again, I/they are doing this with permission. And the difference is that *you* lower the boundaries as per your choice, not have them knocked down by someone else's disregard for them.

One thing about boundaries is that you get to say what is *not* allowed to happen, but you are not allowed to say what *will* happen. So you can say, 'You can only phone between 2.00 and 2.30' (i.e. they cannot phone outside those times, in effect), but you cannot say, 'You must phone me then'. That would be imposing on the other person's freedoms. (This, funnily enough, is something narcissistic mothers themselves fail to grasp.)

In the next letter we'll discuss how to enforce and keep these boundaries, which is not at all easy with a narcissist.

Hugs,

Danu

More about boundaries

Dear DONM …

The thing is that narcissists hate boundaries. They hate them with a passion. They feel attacked by them. How DARE you tell them what they can do and can't do? That's an absolute assault. And so they feel justified in reacting with major force. They'll do whatever they need to do in order to knock that boundary down. They might rage at you until you remove the boundary. Or they might just ignore the boundary and dare you to challenge them (and woe betide you if you do challenge them. Cue narcissistic rage).

So what do you do?

One option is to let them away with it. To never have boundaries with them. To let them call over whenever they like, phone whenever they like, ask you any questions they want, no matter how personal – and you answer them too! That is definitely the easier option. That'll keep the peace for you.

But at what cost?

The cost of your own self-esteem. Your own space. Your own authority to make your own decisions about your own life. Your own privacy. Your own thoughts. Your autonomy.

All of those things are valuable, and it will cost you those to keep the peace. If you are prepared for that price, then it's fine. You understand that I have no opinion about what you do in this case, no attachment to you taking any particular path? I'm simply attempting to lay out the options and the pros and cons of each.

So, yes, keep going as you always have been, if that is your choice, and know the price you are paying. It may well be worth it, and I mean that genuinely, it is not snide sarcasm.

The other option is to start putting boundaries in place, such as the ones on the list you may have written. In each case, create a consequence for her breaking the boundary. It needs to be a consequence that's in your power to enact. Leaving her presence and/or hanging up the phone are good ones.

In each case the magic trick is to carry out the consequence regardless of how she tries to wriggle out of it. Here is an example:

You state the boundary calmly. If the boundary continues to be broken you tell her the consequences of breaking it. (You either do it ahead of time: 'Mum, I am not happy with you always going on about my weight, and I'm asking you now to stop doing that whenever we meet.' Or you do it in the moment, the next time she mentions your weight.)

She may huff and puff and invalidate in one of the many ways narcissists have: 'Oh you're ridiculous, I am only trying to HELP', or 'You can't take a joke!', or similar.

She may cry and sob (especially if the other tricks don't work), 'Oh you're so mean, it's not fair', etc., etc.

Whatever she says, you ignore it. You don't get caught up in discussion about it (because your boundaries are not open for discussion, especially not discussion aimed at derailing).

You just say calmly, 'That may be so, but the fact remains that I am asking you now to stop mentioning my weight.' Or, if she's crying, 'I'm sorry you're upset, but the fact remains that I'm asking you now to stop mentioning my weight'.

If she continues mentioning your weight regardless, you tell her the consequence: 'Mum, I am asking you to stop speaking of my weight. If you do not, I will leave/hang up whenever you speak of it.'

Likewise, if she escalates to a row, you say, 'Mum, I'm going to have to ask you to stop shouting at me, or I will have to leave/hang up/ask you to leave.'

And then, when she continues, as she most likely will, you do exactly what you said: you leave/hang up, etc.

And then, the next time, you do it again.

What you are doing is literally training her, like we train a dog, with consequences. And she doesn't have to like it – in fact, it's guaranteed that she won't. But that's okay. If one of you has to be unhappy, it doesn't have to be you.

Your narcissistic mother will fight and scream and object, make no mistake. She will fight this with everything she's got.

To her, this boundary, which thwarts *her* desire, feels like an attack, like the end of the world in a way which I don't think normal people can really understand.

Her upset will be the greatest the first few times you do this. It's like disciplining a spoiled child or untrained puppy – they won't like the new regime, and will fight it and challenge it every way they can, until they learn you mean it and won't give in to their tactics. This is why it's essential to stay strong and consistent when you do this.

But two things about all of this: firstly, she will learn, regardless, once you are consistent about enforcing the consequences. And secondly, in truth, 'everything she's got' isn't much, when it comes down to it. It's upset and bluster and rage. It's noise and fury, is all. (Unless, of course, she's physically violent and or controls you financially, in which case none of this advice about boundaries applies and you need to sort it out as you would with any violent person.)

I know that this is all scary stuff. The prospect of standing up to your mother when she bullied you all your life can be overwhelming. As ever, I recommend EFT to help you deal with that fear.

One last thing to note – most likely, she'll constantly push the boundary, trying to get you to drop it, or trying to cheat. She might mention a celebrity who's put on a lot of weight and give you a sly look, daring you to react to that. And if she gets away with that, then she'll try something a bit closer to home, and see how far she can push it. It is exhausting, but you will have to keep enforcing the boundaries, or go back to square one. Ahhh, the joys of dealing with a narcissist.

It's also very possible she'll go into full-blown narcissistic rage. We talk about that next.

Hugs,

Danu

Dealing with narcissistic rage

Dear DONM …

Narcissistic rage is the absolute temper that narcissists get into when they have been thwarted or otherwise upset. Given that narcissists are really just small children in an adult body, then we can truly and accurately call these tantrums.

That's all they are, you know, the same tantrums that toddlers have.

But whereas we are able to deal with the child's tantrum – well, even that can be difficult sometimes – it is much harder to deal with the tantrum of the narcissistic mother.

This is because we have been sensitised all our life to be scared of her. We have been trained to fear her rage. Even though we are adults now, when she starts on this rage we still go to the flight or fright response. Our body tenses, our stomach churns, our throat gets dry; in short, all the symptoms of extreme stress. This is called *the flight or fright response*, but one of the other responses in that pattern is to freeze, and that's what happens to us, usually. We learned early that we could not fight, and as a child we could not flee, so our learned response is to freeze.

Not surprisingly, we will do anything we can to avoid this horrible experience. This is why so many of us tend to put up with such bad behaviour from our narcissistic mothers. Which is why, even if we know what we want to do, we often don't do it. To continue the example when I spoke of Rule 1, we may well know that we do not want to spend our birthday with her, but it is just too difficult to face up to the rage and upset that she will inflict upon us if we choose that option.

So, how to deal with it?

When you feel the panic and stress, remind yourself that that is an old pattern. That it is based on beliefs about what she can do to you. Yes, it is true that when you were a child, her anger was very dangerous to you as she really could inflict damage on you or, even if she never did, that possibility was always there.

And as children we are dependent upon our parents for our very survival, so her anger at us was a very real, if primal, threat to our safety.

Now that we are adults, there is nothing, really, that she can do to us.

Now, before I continue in this vein, I need to stress that most narcissistic mothers are not physically violent. Physical violence is not a trait of narcissists as such. It is much more a trait of sociopaths and psychopaths. Having said that, if your mother is likely to be violent and to inflict real damage on you then of course this advice does not apply. You need to take all reasonable steps to defend yourself from physical attack.

Also, if you are in a horrible situation such as your financial well-being being dependent on her (and the narcissistic mothers are very good at contriving such situations), then you might be best not to antagonise her.

But if the violence is 'only' verbal and psychological and emotional, which is the normal narcissistic way, and if you are not dependent on her, then the following should be possible: When she starts her rage just try to step aside a little bit from your emotions about it.

Don't try to deny your emotions, mind. That is essential. You are really feeling them and it is important to validate that. Nothing that I'm telling you is about you invalidating what is going on for you; your mother did enough invalidating all your life, and a large part of the healing journey is that you do validate what is going on for you; you do acknowledge it.

So do not deny that fear that you're feeling, the stress you are feeling. But try to step a little bit aside from it and observe it, and in that way it will lose some of its power.

Also try to observe your mother's behaviour from an emotional distance. (A physical distance would be great too but that might not be possible.) Try to see her rage as the tantrum it is. Observe it as being so pathetic and ridiculous, as it really is. I mean, really, a grown woman throwing a hissy fit because her daughter won't do something small that she wanted her to do! This is ridiculous by any standards.

So try to observe, try to be objective, and in this way it will lose a lot of its power over you. Perhaps even observe it as if you are an anthropologist observing a different culture in that you are clear and present and observing it, but you are not involved in it.

The thing is though, that no matter how much you recognise all this on a logical, rational basis, well your body doesn't know that. You know it's true, but you don't feel it's true.

And so, as ever, I offer you EFT. EFT will change your feelings about this at a core level, so that you feel calm and detached whenever she throws a tantrum. You can use EFT when you are on your own, to build up your resistance to her rage.

I repeat, you were programmed to fear her. But it does not have to stay like that.

Next I'll share some hints and tips for how to react if she's in narcissistic rage.

Hugs,

Danu

When she's in full-blown narcissistic rage

Dear DONM ...

We're going to explore some ideas of what to say to her in the moment when she's in a rage. Note that these are only ideas, that you know your own mother best, and that you need to be mindful always of your own safety.

That said, here are some suggestions.

You're probably stuck doing things you've already agreed to do, but this is for new arrangements. So if she says happily, 'Oh your birthday's soon! What'll we do for it? I always wanted to go to x place, let's do that!', how do you deal with that?

The motto, 'Never explain; never apologise,' is a good one here. You can by all means say 'sorry' as a conversational sop, but don't genuinely apologise as you aren't doing anything wrong. And don't explain (i.e. give reasons/make excuses) because she'll no doubt erode whatever explanation you give. So, 'I can't spend my birthday with you because I promised Jane I'd spend it with her,' will get you:

'But Jane doesn't love you as much as I do, and what did she do for you that I didn't, and that's so unfair, because you spent x other occasion with Jane, and Jane always comes before me ...', etc., etc..

So if at all possible, just say casually, 'I'm afraid I won't be able to spend my birthday with you. But maybe we can meet the following Saturday to celebrate it if you like,' if you're happy to give her a consolation prize. If not, don't say anything about that bit. Just try to change the subject onto talking about her: 'I'm afraid I won't be able to spend my birthday with you after all. Oh, did you get a new dress? It's beautiful on you!'

It's possible she'll be diverted, just as a toddler can be, especially as your new topic of conversation is about her.

But it's equally possible she won't be.

If she says, 'Why not?!', just say calmly, 'I have other plans' – and try again to change the subject. If she persists, maybe try using a technique out of the brilliant book *How to Talk So Kids Will Listen, And Listen So Kids Will Talk*. It's about how to parent well, as you'd guess from the title. And since our narcissistic mothers are children at heart, many of the techniques in this can be tried with them.

The one I'm suggesting here is to reflect their feelings back to them. Say something like, 'I can see you're very upset about that. I can imagine you're very frustrated and hurt by this.'

And she might snap, 'Yes I am! That my own daughter won't spend her birthday with me. The anniversary of the day, let me remind you, that I spent thirteen hours in labour, in agony!'

Don't engage in her specific points, because that way lies defeat. Just say something like, 'Yes, I can see you're very hurt all right' – not patronisingly, genuinely. This is reflecting her emotions back to her. Validating them, really. Her emotions are very real to her, no matter how unjustified they are. (And in fact, I suspect that narcissists, like toddlers, feel things even more strongly than the rest of us as they have no control over their emotions.) So, real and true validation is a very powerful thing.

You can say things like, 'I'm sorry that you're feeling so upset'. This might sound like a contradiction of what I said above, to never apologise, but it's not really. An apology would be to concede that she has more right over your birthday plans than you do, and therefore you're wrong to claim those rights for yourself. So if you say, 'I'm sorry I can't be with you on my birthday', that would be an apology. But 'I'm sorry you're upset' is using the other meaning of 'I'm sorry', the one that means more, 'I'm sad about the fact that ...'.

So, what I'm saying is, don't be sucked into discussing your decision to spend your birthday elsewhere, but do try to comfort her about her upset without taking responsibility for it.

If she refuses to calm down, then you might consider saying calmly, 'I am sorry that you are upset. It's clear that I'm upsetting you more. I'll leave/hang up now and let you gather yourself. Do give me a call when you feel up to talking about it calmly.' (This last sentence is important as you're clearly leaving the ball in her court.)

I know this sounds almost blasphemous. For sure it's changing the whole pattern of your encounters. But, either the dynamic changes, or everything stays the same and you remain under her thumb. Which, honestly, is a fully valid option. You understand that I am not advocating rebellion? That would not be my place at all. Sometimes the path of least resistance is the right one. You might not be in a position to stand up to her and change the dynamic. And that's quite all right.

But if you *are* in a position to change the dynamic, and you're tired living your life as her chew-toy, and you want to incorporate Rule 1 (Do What You Want To Do) in your life ... well then, by definition, your behaviour has to change. Her behaviour surely won't – why would it, when up until now it has got her all she wants!

And yes, she won't like it. But that's okay. Remember: *If one of you has to be upset, it doesn't have to be you.*

As I said earlier, her upset will be the greatest the first few times you do this until she learns better.

Be prepared for tantrums – just deal with those as suggested above.

She might stop talking to you to try to guilt you into crawling back to her. And that often works. Their silence is very powerful for as long as we let it be. But if you can see it as the manipulation it is, then you have the choice of letting it continue. See who blinks first. It's very likely that she will crack first, when her need for your attention becomes stronger than her need to ignore you.

Most likely she'll contact you most cheerfully, with no reference to all that went before, as if you parted in great form only a day or two previously. It's probably best, especially if you got your way, to play along with that and just carry on.

None of it is easy. I know that. But it is doable, and in that lies your power.

Hugs,

Danu

What if she cries?

Dear DONM …

If rage doesn't work, she might well turn to tears. This was certainly my own mother's tactic, and I know she's not alone. If she can't gain your fear, she may well make a play for your sympathy. She might sob something like, 'Oh it's so unfair! You always hurt me. After all I've done for you. It hurts so much that my own daughter doesn't want to spend her birthday with me,' etc., etc..

What do you do then? In many ways this is harder to deal with than her rage. You feel like such a monster. You feel so guilty and horrible, a bad, awful, nasty person to upset your mother like this. She was right with everything she said about you, wasn't she?

The thing is, though, that this is just pure manipulation. She wants her way and she'll do everything she can to get it. I don't deny that there's genuine emotion in there too, as she has been thwarted in getting what she wants and is genuinely upset about that. But it's all designed to make you cave in to her wishes.

I know the pull is very strong when she does this, the need or desire to placate her, to calm her, to make the tears stop. And so you might well give in to her. And that's okay if you do. Don't beat yourself up about it. She has been playing this game a long time and she's very good at it, and it's totally understandable that you would concede.

But, maybe think ahead of time what you might do in the case of tears, and come up with a plan. You might choose to know that disappointment comes to us all, and that it's not your job to protect her from that. You might choose to know that she is choosing this upset, or certainly the scale of it, and that is up to her, and not your responsibility. You might choose to be strong, and even hard, in the cause of your own wishes, needs, and desires. You are fully entitled to do this, once your original choice was an ethical and fair one. Which I'm sure it was. You wouldn't expect to celebrate your birthday instead of supporting her through a major operation, I bet. In these examples we're talking about honouring your wishes above her whims.

And so you could choose to comfort her for her genuine upset, and call her bluff in a way for her manipulative upset. You could honour her tears without conceding to her desires. 'I'm sorry you're upset, Mum,' you might say. 'I can see you're disappointed.' But if she sobs something like, 'I'd stop crying if only you agreed to do what I want', or hints at that – well, you can remain kind and strong at the same time. Witness her tears and comfort them without giving in to them. It is the same as if you had a child crying because she couldn't have chocolate for dinner; you could empathise and comfort about her upset, but you wouldn't even consider giving into what she wanted because it would not be right. The same applies here.

Hugs,

Danu

The silent treatment

Dear DONM …

So, narcissistic rage is one tactic, and tears is another, and yet another is to ignore you. To sulk, basically. To effectively banish you from her presence until you cave in and give in to her.

Especially if you say kindly and calmly, 'I'll leave now; do get back in touch when you're able to discuss it calmly'; well, she might not get in touch at all.

This is a surprisingly powerful action. None of us likes to be banished. None of us wants to live in that limbo where she's not talking to us, where she's angry with us.

Or, the silence can be portrayed by her and/or understood by us, to be because she is so hurt at our sheer cruelty to her, and we hate making her so miserable.

So this tactic often works to bring us to heel. To have us ringing and apologising even though we did nothing wrong. To do whatever it takes to get back into her good books, no matter the cost to our own autonomy and our own self-esteem. Or to do whatever it takes to stop her pain, no matter how much it is self-inflicted.

But the thing is – her silent treatment is an empty gesture on her behalf. It ONLY has the impact and value and weight that we give it. She's banking on that. And we can choose to either *ignore* the impact it has on us, or to *erase* the impact it has on us.

To ignore it, you can feel the fear and stress and upset of it all, just as you always did if this happened before. But you allow those feelings to be felt, fully, without judgement, without resistance. Allow them to turn up, to live for a while in your body. It's uncomfortable, but it's not dangerous in any way. And a lot of the discomfort about it comes from our resistance to the feelings, to our fear about experiencing them, and when we allow them, the resistance and fear is neutralised. And as the feelings are allowed to present themselves, they'll fade and disappear.

So, just feel the feelings without believing you have to act upon them. You can feel dreadful about the fact she's angry with you, or hurting badly, without taking the step (which is nothing less than your complete surrender, don't forget) to stop her being angry with you, or hurt.

You'll have to keep doing this. The feelings will often come back with every thought about her. Every time the phone rings and it's not her, for example. But each time, you can feel the feelings calmly and they will go.

Rather than just ignoring the feelings, you can erase them using EFT. You can tap whenever you feel the stress and the fear, tapping while breathing deeply, until it passes.

The whole situation isn't easy, I know, but you are fighting for nothing less than your own autonomy, don't forget. You are fighting for the right to say no to her, to make your own decisions. This is a battle worth fighting, I think. And this one will be the hardest, as you're changing the rules and she, of course, is resisting it.

So, a battle worth fighting. And your weapon is: to do nothing. Doing nothing might seem like a very passive thing, but in the right situation it is an extremely powerfully proactive action.

You carefully left the ball in her court, so it's up to her to contact you.

Now, you need to know that it's possible that she will never contact you again. It's possible that her anger at your insubordination, or her love of the drama of declaiming your cruelty, or her indifference, might lead her to cut you off completely. You need to think about this and see if you're okay with that outcome. It's a big decision for sure, and I don't seek to influence it. I do throw out the question, however: if someone's presence in your life is wholly dependent upon you obeying them fully, how healthy a relationship is that?

However, it's unlikely she'll let you go. (I mean, unlikely in the sense of what most narcissistic mothers would do, so, statistically unlikely. Obviously I don't know your mother or how she'll react so I can't predict that.) If she's like most narcissistic mothers, she needs you as her source of Narcissistic Supply. (Narcissistic Supply is the name given to narcissists' addiction to attention.) It's most likely therefore that she'll do the Silent Treatment to bring you to heel, and when she realises it isn't working and/or her need for your attention trumps her need to punish you, then she will contact you.

In my own mother's case, it took nine months.

My situation was slightly different in that I knew I didn't want to see her again, and so the silence was good for me rather than troubling. But she didn't know that. All she knew was that we weren't speaking, and she let it go on for nine full months.

If your narcissistic mother does contact you, then I can (almost) guarantee how it'll go. She'll most likely contact you cheerfully, with ZERO reference to all that went before, as if you parted in great form only a day or two previously.

So how do you react?

If you want to keep in contact with her, it's probably best to play along with her cheerful tone. Answer her equally cheerfully and superficially. Make no reference to the previous row. Pretend it never happened. Trying to discuss it so you can come up with a better understanding between you just will not work. She's a narcissist. It'd be like trying to reason with a toddler.

However, be prepared to fight the same battle the next time she wants you to do something you don't want to do. That'll be the crunch event. It could be that the fallout from the first incident exhausted you so much that you want to never go through it again. Which is a perfectly valid response, I do stress that. But it does mean that you're conceding a lifetime of never standing up to her ever. You'll have won the battle and lost the war.

There is good news though. If you do stand up to your mother again, she'll learn that you do mean what you say. This time the Silent Treatment will probably last a much shorter period of time, if it happens at all. And you're well on your way to reclaiming your autonomy. Go you!

Hugs,

Danu

Flying Monkeys swoop in

Dear DONM ...

During the Silent Treatment, your mother might send in the Flying Monkeys.

This term comes from *The Wizard Of Oz*, in which the witch sends out these malevolent Flying Monkeys to do her bidding. The Flying Monkeys that your narcissistic mother sends out most likely will not be malevolent, but more likely misguided. They've only heard her side of the story, don't forget. And therefore they're going to plead with you to give in to her.

This Flying Monkey will be someone who's close enough to your mother that they're in the blast zone for her frustration about your intransigence. And by *your intransigence* I mean *your fair boundaries calmly stated and enforced*, of course. But your mother's seeing it as intransigence and the Flying Monkey is repeating the official narrative.

As it's someone close it might be your father, or a sibling, or aunt. Somebody like that. So, very possibly, someone you love, and whose respect you want, and whose well-being you desire.

This person may well genuinely love you and want good things for you too. But if they're caught in your narcissistic mother's web (and they are, or they wouldn't be doing this), then what they want even more than that is your mother to have her way. This could be because that'll give them a quiet life, or because they have genuinely been convinced of her side of the story. Or both, of course, along with possibly even other reasons. People are complex.

So they do not have your best interests at heart, no matter how much they present themselves that way.

They have a mission to bring you back into the fold on your narcissistic mother's terms, no matter the personal cost to you. And they'll do whatever it takes to do that.

They might use scolding: 'How can you be so mean to your mother?' They might use guilt: 'She's so upset you know. She's crying all the time.' Or variations of those.

So how do you deal with it?

You can either say, 'I'm not going to discuss my mother with you' (phrased more gently than that if needed, of course); or simply, 'She's the one not talking to me, you know. I asked her to contact me when she was ready.'

They might say, 'Well, why don't you be the bigger person and contact her. She's too upset to contact you.'

Don't fall for that! More about being the bigger person later, but for now just don't fall for it!

Just repeat, 'Well, she knows she is welcome to contact me whenever she wants.'

If they insist, trying to get you to contact her, then they are stepping on your boundaries big time and need to be stopped. You can say something like, 'I do appreciate your concern. But this is between me and her and so I'd prefer if we didn't discuss it any further.'

And then do what you need to in order to enforce that. In a very real way you'll be doing with the Flying Monkey what you did with your mother: stating fair boundaries and calmly enforcing them.

Sometimes the Flying Monkey will beg you to contact your narcissistic mother on the grounds that: 'She's taking it out on me, and I can't bear it any more.'

This is a tough one for sure. You don't want the Flying Monkey suffering. But here's the thing – it's not *you* making them suffer, but your mother. The Flying Monkey is responsible for their own relationship with your mother; you are not responsible for that.

And listen to what they're really saying: 'Can you please continue to suffer from her treatment so I don't have to?' Is that a fair thing to ask?

This might be the time to tell the Flying Monkey the truth about her, so they understand. But maybe not – do read back on the letter about telling your siblings about Narcissistic Personality Disorder, before you make any decision.

The bottom line with Flying Monkeys though is that you are under no obligation to listen to them. Your mother's having sent them is just more manipulation (no matter if she directly asked them to come, or, more likely, manipulated the situation so they'd do it of their own accord). And it's both unfair *of* them and *on* them to do this, and you are fully entitled not to facilitate this.

Be aware though that if you stand up to Flying Monkeys they might well cut you off too, preferring to stand firmly in your mother's camp. (*sigh* All this because you didn't want to spend your birthday with her. But that's how these hideous dynamics go ....)

More about this next.

Hugs,

Danu

Losing the Flying Monkeys too

Dear DONM …

Be aware that the narcissistic mothers cleverly weave a very tight co-dependent web of their relationships. I do visualise it as a literal web – with her the big, fat, malevolent spider in the middle, and everyone else stuck to the threads, trapped, arrayed around her. Some of those people will be struggling to get free (you, maybe), and others will be sitting quietly, acquiescent and accepting. Those others perhaps cannot even imagine their lives free, can't visualise a life lived without being in constant reference to her and her needs and moods and sulks and whims. They are comfortable with the status quo, as people tend to be, and are terrified of change.

And so if you make changes by standing up to your mother, you may well terrify them. Not only may they be suffering because she is taking her anger at you out on them, or inflicting her dramatic *back-of-hand-to-forehead-and-take-to-the-chaise-longue-with-the-smelling-salts* hurt onto them, but you're also rocking their boat too. You're upsetting the balance that has sustained them (no matter how poorly) all this time.

They hate this, understandably.

And so, they might become annoyed with you too. It's far safer to be angry with you than to be angry with your mother. And in a way they are justified in being angry with you – you *are* the one making changes, after all.

And so, there is a very real risk that if they are forced to choose between you and your mother, they'll choose your mother. Of course, you will not be the one forcing the choice; your mother will be. But she might well do that. She might say to them, 'Well if you're going to continue seeing [you], then I want nothing to do with you.' And they would have to choose her, unless they're able to break free entirely.

So, you do risk losing other people close to you by this process. It's unfair. It's completely and utterly unfair. All you wanted to do was spend your birthday your way, after all.

Something totally simple, that most people take for granted. Something absolutely reasonable. And now all this. But that's the way of it when you have a narcissistic mother and co-dependent family.

Only you can decide if it's worth it.

The thing is that in a way it's not easy to make the decision now. You're probably still stuck to the web. You don't know how good life in freedom is. Take my word, and the experience of so many other DONMs – it is so worth it. Yes, there's a price to pay, and often it's a very high price. But *freeDONM* is wonderful and liberating and empowering and all sorts of good things.

Hugs,

Danu

Being the bigger person

Dear DONM …

So, Flying Monkeys have the mission to bring you back into the fold on your narcissistic mother's terms, no matter the personal cost to you. And so they'll do whatever it takes.

And one of the favourite tactics seems to be something along the lines of:

'Yes, I know she's being unreasonable. But you know what she's like. So, come on, be the bigger person here. Tell her you're sorry even though we both know you did nothing wrong, but it'll make her happy and we can all get along again.'

Be the bigger person. Right.

Be the bigger person, with the implication that if you hold your position then you're a small person, a narrow, bigoted, petty person. That the mature thing to do is to pander to her. It won't take much after all – just a pro-forma apology in the interests of keeping the family together. It's not so much to ask, is it?

Put like that, it's hard to refute. And especially, as I've already said, when it comes from someone you love.

What do you do?

With always the caveat that you should do what *you* decide, and not based on anything I say, I think that you need to know that you have no obligation to fall for this.

You might choose to concede. That's your right of course. But you have no obligation to.

In a way that the Flying Monkey most likely will not appreciate, *you are already being the bigger person*. You are being the one who is big enough (i.e. adult enough) to state and enforce a calm boundary. You are the one being mature enough to step outside dysfunction and manipulation, to stop playing toxic games. To say: I do not wish to do x and I will not.

And that even if that were not so, you have no obligation to be the bigger person. In healthy relationships people are equally big.

And that 'being the bigger person' is just a euphemism for

'let her continue to treat you exactly as she wishes while you roll over and take it', and you have no obligation whatsoever to do that.

The Flying Monkey is being disingenuous to dress that up as some kind of virtue. And even more disingenuous to dress it up in their concern for your mother when it is most likely about their own wish to no longer experience the fallout of your mother's drama and fury.

And you are perfectly within your rights to say calmly to the Flying Monkey, 'I don't need to be a bigger person if it means apologising for something I didn't do. I appreciate you trying to sort it out, but this is between her and me and it's best left that way.'

It's totally your right to establish boundaries with the Flying Monkey just as much as with your narcissistic mother.

Hugs,

Danu

What about your other relationships?

Dear DONM …

As you grow and heal from your narcissistic upbringing, you might experience pushback from people around you. Not just from your narcissistic mother (if you're still in touch with her) or her Flying Monkeys, but from other people as well. Your significant other or partner, for example. Or best friends. Or colleagues.

They may start complaining about you. 'I don't know what's got into you. You're being awful snarky lately.' Or even, 'You're being very selfish lately.'

There are two possibilities here.

The first is that, unfortunately, that relationship is toxic too. I am sorry to say this as I know it's not easy to hear. (And it might not be so anyway; see below.) But the fact is that DONMs can often find themselves in other abusive relationships. It's what we know, after all. It's what we're trained for. And abusers can find us to be good fodder, and are attracted to us for that reason.

And of course an abuser isn't going to want you to find your power and so will do all in their power to try to put you back in your box when you start becoming assertive.

The second possibility is that they are not abusers at all. But even so they are threatened by the changes in you. It makes sense: they fell in love with you/got to know you as you were, and here you are changing.

They liked the old way better.

They liked being able to have things their way all the time, and don't want that to change. That's understandable, and even decent non-abusive people can struggle with that.

Also, change is scary for people, even good change. And this is change they haven't chosen, and are not steering, and they don't know where they'll end up. They might fear that you will leave them if this carries on, that you might outgrow them.

No wonder they resist that change, and maybe even try to sabotage it.

And you know, they might be right about you outgrowing them. Once you start to grow and stretch, you most likely won't want to shrink to fit ever again. You start to expect more, and better. And sometimes even genuine well-meaning people cannot provide that.

So, there are lots of reasons why those close to you might resist your growth. You need to decide if you want to continue growing regardless of their resistance. Not in a nasty-selfish way, but in a birthright kind of way. But it's a valid choice to stay small, to not rock the boat. I do not advocate one or the other as that wouldn't be my place; I just want to lay out the possibilities and potential issues for you.

So, those who are near to you might resist your growth, either because they're abusers or because they're ordinary, scared people. Don't be surprised if that happens, and maybe have a think ahead of time about how you'll react if/when they do.

The harsh fact is that you might find that some relationships die during this process.

My own marriage ended after I cut off contact with my parents. The No Contact gave me space to look at a marriage that, frankly, had never worked. We both (me more than him I have to say, but him too), had been trying to salvage the unsalvageable since forever.

It was never an abusive relationship; that was good luck rather than good planning as I was well primed for emotional abuse. But my ex was, and is, a fundamentally decent man. However our marriage was dysfunctional (as in, not-working) from Day 1. And it was horrendously co-dependent, looking back.

And so my marriage ended as part of this journey. And other relationships have ended too.

This has been so painful. The past years have been absolute hell for me in so many ways. And I cannot promise that, once on this path, the same or similar won't happen to you too.

But you know what, I wouldn't change a thing. The price has been horrendous, but the gifts have been beyond wonderful.

I'm so much stronger now, so much better balanced. I'm learning and growing and increasing in happiness and peace. And I believe things will continue to get better too, as the worst of the upheaval is over and I start to reap more benefits of the growth. The changes are intoxicating in their possibilities, and so empowering.

Yes, a data point of one (i.e. me) is not statistically significant. But it is all I have to share after all. I haven't conducted a whole study on this. And you need to make your decisions for you, and I wish you courage and fortitude for those decisions. The problem is that you have to pay the price without knowing the rewards. The caterpillar cannot envisage what it is like to be a butterfly, and how she will fly free and beautiful, even as her body liquefies to a pulp first.

I just know that I love flying, and I love my bright colourful wings.

Hugs,

Danu

More about guilt

Dear DONM …

You may not be long on this journey before you consider cutting down contact as much as possible with your narcissistic mother (known as Low Contact), or even cutting off contact with her entirely (known as No Contact).

There is a lot of information about these topics in *You're Not Crazy*, but what I want to talk about now is how you *feel* about all of this. If you are like most DONMs you will feel a huge guilt at even the prospect of cutting down contact or cutting off contact.

This is totally understandable. There are a lot of strands conspiring to make you feel like this. Apart from Stockholm Syndrome (also known as Trauma Bonding) as discussed in *You're Not Crazy*, there are four other strands that I can see.

The first is your own mother's brainwashing, which makes you feel responsible for her. (We'll be talking a lot more about this.) The second is your love for her, if you have that. The third is your desire to please her and keep her happy and maybe win her love that way. The fourth is society's attitude towards mothers: society reveres mothers, it puts them on a pedestal, and woe betide the woman who dares to say the Emperor has no clothes or the mother is not perfect.

I have read an observation that society's need to believe in the mother-myth is so strong that our fairy-tales feature bad stepmothers, not mothers. That these ancient stories wanted to explore the topic of bad mothers, but could not do so directly.

And nowadays anyone who dares to say that she is not in touch with her mother gets a metaphorical (or maybe even literal) hissing intake of breath, as the disapproval is plainly shown. It's hard to go against that. I remember being on a radio interview when *You're Not Crazy* first came out, and I explained how it was an abusive relationship, and that's why I left it. And even after all that, the presenter asked me at the end would I not try to sort things out with my mother.

I said, 'If you had a woman on your show who had an abusive partner, and after years and years of trying to sort things out, and being beaten down at every turn, had finally managed to escape from him, would you ask her about trying to sort things out with him?'

The presenter, to his credit, got immediately what I was saying, and conceded that he would not.

But society doesn't acknowledge that there can be abusive mother-daughter relationships, and so to admit that you are not in touch with your mother (or only in rare contact, in limited circumstances) is absolute heresy.

All this adds to the feelings of guilt. And that guilt can keep you trapped in this abusive relationship.

And this is an abusive relationship, make no mistake. If your mother is narcissistic, a healthy loving mutually supportive relationship is not possible.

But you might know that logically, but not feel it.

The guilt you feel *is real*. I do not invalidate it. It's very real. *But it is not true*. It is not justified. Guilt is for when we do something wrong, and protecting yourself from an abuser can never be wrong. Yes, that abuser might be dressed up as your mother, wearing a pretty mask, fooling society and even you. But she's still an abuser.

I suggest that when you feel the guilt, you observe it as if from a safe distance. It's a bit of a psychological trick which is very helpful and very doable. Observing an emotion helps distance you from it a bit, rather than swimming, and even drowning, in it. Notice that you are feeling this guilt. Take the time to find out where in your body that guilt is sitting. What size is it? Shape? Texture? (It will have a location in your body, and when you examine it, a size, shape and texture.)

The guilt feels like your enemy, making you feel bad. But it is actually your friend, trying to help you, trying to make sure you don't do the wrong thing. It just has wrong information about what the wrong thing is. So – and this may sound really silly, in fact I'm sure it does! – I recommend that you talk to the guilt. The guilt is a part of your brain, so it's really you talking to you, so it's not as mad as it sounds. And say something like: 'Guilt, I know you are trying to help me here by making me feel bad for cutting off contact with my mother. But there is no need for me to feel guilty, I promise you. You have false information. I am doing nothing wrong here. I ask you to let go of the guilt now.'

Over time the feelings of guilt should fade.

One way, of course, of speeding up this process, is to use EFT.

Whichever way you do this, I do invite you to free yourself from the untrue guilt – you deserve no less.

Hugs,

Danu

The need to belong

Dear DONM …

The need for humans to belong is very very strong. Indeed, psychologist Abraham Maslow in his famous Hierarchy of Needs put the need to belong as one of our highest needs, just behind survival needs such as safety, food and shelter.

This makes perfect sense of course. For most of human history, belonging to a tribe was an essential survival strategy. This is because we are weak and defenceless alone, and it is only as part of a tribe that we can survive.

Even now a human would struggle to survive without the help and infrastructure provided by other humans. Technically, in this more formal world, we could survive with only the help and assistance of strangers.

But it doesn't feel like that – we still *feel* the need for our tribe.

In this way, the need to belong is not AFTER the other survival needs – it is *another* survival need.

No wonder we feel it so strongly.

But DONMs then have a big problem with that. We often feel that we do not belong anywhere at all. It is understandable as we, in a very real sense, did not belong in our own families. We were not welcome there, we were not cherished and nurtured as a valuable and important family member. No wonder we struggle sometimes to belong in the world.

Or rather, to *feel* as if we belong in the world.

Because we *do* belong in the world, just as much as anyone else.

I think this sense of not belonging can be a self-fulfilling prophecy in ways.

We believe we don't belong, that we're not good enough – and somehow we project that belief and others pick up on it and react to it. Now, this is only my own theory, I have to stress, based on my own experiences.

I used EFT to make me feel that I belonged better in group

situations, and it did change my experiences in groups. Whether people literally responded better to me, or whether I just felt they did (and maybe they had never responded badly, maybe that was just my perception), didn't seem to matter. I felt that I belonged there, and that's what seemed to happen.

So I offer you to use EFT for this. Feeling like you belong makes a big difference to so many experiences, and it's well worth pursuing. And in truth, it's no less than we deserve.

Hugs,

Danu

Self-care struggles

Dear DONM …

One of the worst aspects of the DONM legacy is that often we don't look after ourselves properly. We either neglect our own self-care, or we actively sabotage ourselves. The punishment can take forms like nail-biting or eating the wrong foods, or be as severe as self-cutting.

I know I used to struggle with basic self-care. I did it, don't get me wrong. The desire to be socially acceptable made sure of that. But I had to force myself to do it. It was like climbing a mountain every single time. It was exhausting. And taking all that energy to do really basic stuff, meant that I had that much less energy left for actually living.

I think it's understandable when you've been raised as we have. Especially if you had an Ignoring Mother who neglected your care needs. The message deeply ingrained is: 'You're not worth looking after. You don't deserve to have your self-care needs met. You're not valuable enough to be minded.'

And then, when we reach adulthood, we take over her job for her. It's a perversion of the normal situation. In a healthy situation the mother minds the child until the child is big enough, and then the mother hands over the job of minding the child to the child, and the child takes on that job. It all happens very naturally and gradually, with ever-increasing amounts of responsibility handed to the child as she's ready for them.

The same thing happens to us, but, as I say, in a perverted way. The narcissistic mother's 'job' is to neglect and abuse us, and she hands that over to us, and we naturally and without realising it, accept the job. It's all we know, and all we think we're worth.

When I say 'think', it's not that we rationalise this or do it on a conscious level. It's all on a very subconscious level. But the result is the same: we take over her job of neglecting ourselves or abusing ourselves.

That training, that indoctrination, runs deep, and it's a

place where I think EFT comes into its own. I try to offer other alternatives to EFT where possible, because I don't want to just always push EFT or make it seem like the only option. But in this case I have not found anything that works as well to change such deeply-entrenched indoctrination.

Whatever you decide, I do hope you find it easier to care for yourself, as you truly deserve that.

Hugs,

Danu

What about your happiness?

Dear DONM …

Happiness is something that's often been on my mind. I think it's probably something that's on everybody's mind. Happiness is what we humans seek, after all. All of us, not just DONMs. And we seek it in objects and experiences and relationships.

The trick, I know, is to feel happy regardless of external circumstances. Far easier said than done; it's a journey I'm still on, one during which I stumble often.

The Buddhists are right, I think, in that it's attachment which causes suffering. There is only one thing that makes me unhappy – that I want something and cannot have it. Whether that's my mother's love, or a healthy family dynamic, or something trivial like a new dress, it is the mismatch between *wanting it* and *not having it* which makes me unhappy.

One solution is to get every single thing we want. But of course that's not a realistic solution. Many things, such as wanting love from a narcissistic mother, are out of our hands to obtain. Others, such as material goods are limited due finances, but in truth they don't make us really happy even if we get them, as we always want the next thing.

The other option, the Buddhist one, is to release all desires. If you didn't want anything, ever, you wouldn't be unhappy.

I'm not sure that that works either. Even if we *could* release all desires, is that really ideal? It is part of the richness of our human experience to want, to desire, to aspire, to seek. We'd all be still living in caves, otherwise.

And so the trick, I believe, is to separate our happiness from our desires. Have desires, by all means, and strive to reach them. But not to make happiness conditional upon reaching them.

I think I'm trying to say that it's a good goal to have happiness and desires be on parallel paths, rather than intertwined. For them to be independent of each other.

As it is, we put conditions on happiness. 'I'll be happy when

I get x' is the thinking. But the corollary of that is that we can't be happy unless we have x.

And it's never-ending. Say we get x. It will make us happy – that is true. But only for a while. A very interesting study found that really good events like winning the lottery, and really bad events like becoming paralysed, did indeed respectively raise, and lower, the happiness levels, just as you'd expect. But, interestingly: only temporarily. After a year the happiness levels of the individuals concerned were back to where they had been before that life-changing event. And if the impact of such huge events as that last only a year, how much less would the impact of smaller events last?

And so we'd get used to having x, and now be unhappy because we don't have y. It's never-ending.

And so, the way to end it is to, as I'm suggesting, unhook happiness from these desires. To stop putting conditions on happiness. This takes discipline and intention, but is, I am convinced, a path worth taking. In a very real way we simply make the decision to be happy in our lives as they are. Easier said than done of course, but it truly is only a decision away. And this is a bit do-as-I-say-not-as-I-do, as I struggle with this one. I know it is possible though, as I have done it at times and it feels so good. I do have to keep re-making the decision, falling off the happiness wagon and then climbing back on. Perhaps one day I'll be able to make the final decision, but for now I know it is good to aspire to and to try to do.

The topic of looking for happiness applies to everybody, but DONMs have specific challenges too, so we'll be discussing those next.

Hugs,

Danu

More about happiness

Dear DONM ...

We spoke about separating our desires from our happiness – making our happiness unconditional in other words.

But there is one other issue that, it seems to me, comes up for DONMs.

Often it can seem dangerous to be happy. Not right. Stressful, as though some doom is going to fall because we're happy.

This can apply to DONMs whose mothers didn't like them being happy, and took steps to make sure that they weren't happy.

These mothers were (are) threatened by their daughter's happiness. A happy daughter is not 100 per cent focused on her mother for a start, as she's living her life and enjoying her happiness. And if she's not 100 per cent focussed on her mother, that's a lack of Narcissistic Supply for the mother. A happy daughter is also not as fearful or as biddable.

And so, these mothers would have taken steps to ensure that their daughters didn't experience happiness – or at least, not for long.

They might say things like, 'Wipe that smile off your face or I'll wipe it off for you.'

They might have launched into a tirade, a rage, a row in order to spoil the happy mood.

Or they might, and this is the nastiest of them all, take away the source of their daughters' happiness.

The beloved puppy was given away. The ride to dance lessons disappeared so the dancing had to stop. The new friend was bad-mouthed enough that the friendship withered.

The tactics would vary of course, but the end result is the same – a daughter who subconsciously, and totally reasonably, believes that it is not safe to be happy.

The effect of this belief is that we cannot allow ourselves to be happy. Which makes perfect sense, right? If it's not safe to be happy, we'd be crazy to let ourselves do the dangerous thing.

We very possibly feel stressed whenever we start to be happy – but this feeling is so normal and common that we don't even identify it as such. The result is that we damp down the happy feelings.

Or, we might even subconsciously sabotage the things that make us happy, just as our mother did. And there's a kind of irony in that, isn't there? We might be perfectly capable of getting ourselves to dance lessons now that we're adult, but somehow we just stop going.

This is so, so sad, when we carry on our mother's role of abusing us. Our motivation is completely different, of course. But the result is the same.

As ever, EFT is the way to root out those stale incorrect beliefs, and I offer you to use it if you find yourself feeling stressed or panicked at the thought, or feeling, of happiness. It will leave you able to feel good about feeling happy. Feeling right, and peaceful about that state.

You can use EFT, tapping for the statement, 'It's not safe to feel happiness', and see where that brings you, and tap then using statements that come up for you as you do that. Feeling safe about feeling happy is no more than your birthright, no matter that it was stolen from you. You deserve to reclaim it.

Hugs,

Danu

More about beliefs

Dear DONM …

In *You're Not Crazy* I spoke extensively of how our beliefs impact us hugely. I wish to expand on this now.

The fact is that our beliefs are integral to the quality of our lives.

And *that* is because our beliefs steer us. They're our programming, almost literally. Maybe really literally.

The trouble is that these beliefs are buried so deep down, and are so subtle, that we're not aware of their impact. And therefore we cannot make conscious decisions as to whether to believe our beliefs or not, so to speak

If our beliefs would speak to us clearly at the time, it would be a lot easier.

Say for example somebody invites you to make a presentation to leaders in your industry. If you could have a rational debate with your beliefs they might say to you:

'Yeah, that sounds like a good opportunity for sure. It'd be great to get to speak to them, and would really raise your profile. But the thing is that it isn't safe for you to speak in public. They might laugh at you – they probably *will* laugh at you – if you make even the smallest mistake. Remember how your narcissistic mother always laughed at you when you did that, and how small it always made you feel? You don't want to experience that again, sure you don't?'

You could then calmly consider all that.

And you might respond: 'That's true. Good point. But I'll be able to prepare this speech, so the chances of making any mistakes are minimal. And if I do – well, these people aren't my narcissistic mother. They won't be so petty as to laugh. They'll know I'm not a professional speaker so they won't be judging me on that, but on the quality of my content.'

'And you know,' you might continue as you consider it further, 'if they did laugh then that's okay. It would say far more about them than it does about me. I'm not that helpless child now, so I am strong enough to survive, or even dismiss, their laughter.'

And in this way, you and your beliefs could have a reasoned calm adult discussion, and you could make a balanced decision about whether to give the presentation or not.

Your decision might even be: 'You're right. I don't want to risk that. I'll turn down the opportunity.'

And that'd be okay. Either way it'd be your conscious, considered, decision.

But that's not what happens. What really happens is this:

The offer is made. Your brain hears it and immediately sends it to the Beliefs Vault for evaluation. The belief that it'd be unsafe for you to speak in public would come rushing forward, warning frantically of the danger, and in order to protect you from that danger, your brain floods your system with stress and fear feelings.

All this happens in an instant, so that all you're aware of is the offer to speak followed by instant, unidentified, stress and fear.

And next thing, you hear yourself turning down the offer as a knee-jerk reaction.

Or you agree to do it despite the knots in your stomach, and spend the intervening time feeling ill at the prospect.

When it comes time to do the talk, it might go well and a new belief will be forged, about how you can do these things well.

Or, more likely the belief might remain as you subconsciously think, 'We got away with it that time because you didn't make any mistakes. But the danger still lurks. It could all go wrong the next time.'

Or worse again, humans being what they are, you might even subconsciously sabotage the presentation in some way, to prove to yourself that you were right about it being dangerous.

Do you see how it works? Your *conscious, thinking, rational self* doesn't get to make the decision at all (either to do it or not to do it). Your *beliefs* make the decision for you.

They steer you.

They steer you away from danger as they perceive it. They're your friend, trying to help you. The problem is that their assumptions about what's dangerous go unexamined.

It's very difficult to work against this system as it's so quick, and so subtle.

But, there is good news. By their fruits you shall know them. Every time you want to do something *and* you don't, there is a belief in play.

Also, the more you get used to noticing the feelings and emotions, the more you'll know there's a belief behind them, in play.

And EFT is terrific at exposing those beliefs.

All you do is to tap, in our example, on the statement, 'I want to do the presentation *and* I don't.' And as you tap, the beliefs will come up. The awareness will come to you: 'They might laugh at me'.

And then you tap on that statement: 'They might laugh at me.'

And see what happens then. Either that belief will fade and ease – or the belief behind it, e.g. 'I couldn't bear it if they laughed at me', will come up for examination and erasing using EFT.

And in this way you get to examine all the beliefs which are running your life, and eliminate those which aren't true and don't serve you.

Sometimes the resistance might prove to have a really good reason, or belief, behind it. You might realise that your belief is that you're not ready for such a big presentation, and when you consider it calmly, you realise that, no, you're really not.

And that's okay. This way you're turning down the opportunity for good and considered reasons. In a very real way, you WERE able to have that discussion with your beliefs, and able to make good decisions for good reasons. Nothing about this process is to make you automatically override your beliefs or reactions, but rather to examine them and make a conscious decision taking into account all the facts.

You can also use this process to examine your beliefs as they relate to your narcissistic mother. There might be a belief, 'I have to keep her happy' or 'I cannot cope if she's angry with me'. Are they true? Worth finding out!

Hugs,

Danu

So, were you really born broken?

Dear DONM …

One of the most toxic 'gifts' our narcissistic mother gives us, in my opinion, is the belief (which feels like way more than a belief – it feels like an unquestioned knowing, an absolute truth) that we were born broken. That, from the moment of our birth there was something inherently flawed about us, something wrong, misshapen, grotesque. This is an extremely nasty form of cruelty, to take this perfect little baby and to dump on her all this psychic toxic sludge, so that when she looks in her mental mirror, it is the sludge she sees and not her own innate beauty.

And oh, all our flaws we're told about. I wouldn't mind but in most cases they're not even our real flaws. My own parents didn't even know me well enough to know my real flaws. What they projected onto me was what they needed to project to keep me docile, to keep me 'bad' so she could be 'good'. The flaws of over-sensitivity and bad perceptions, among them.

And worse, there was always the spectre of other flaws, which they knew, and would reveal to me if they needed to. I called it the Horrible Danu Mirror. The threat was always there to show me what I really look like; the toxic sludge being the least of it. And I couldn't bear to see how horrible they found me. My psyche was struggling enough with how horrible I already knew I was; I knew it couldn't cope with learning I was even worse than that. And so I always caved at that threat, climbed back into my box, and let them continue to treat me as they wanted. It was a very powerful weapon in their hands. And of course the fact I caved meant I never called their bluff, never realised they had nothing particularly bad about me, and I was not this gargoyle they tried to convince me I was. (The one time, towards the end of our relationship, when it went far enough that they did share how awful I was, guess what was the horrible thing about me? The fact that when they left my home after visits I closed the door immediately instead of waving until they were out of sight as I should. Seriously.)

No wonder I, and I know other DONMs too, grow up with the absolute belief that we're born broken, that we're intrinsically damaged.

And that's a tough burden to carry constantly. In a way it's like air pressure. We humans don't consciously experience air pressure because we are used to it all our lives. But it's there, pressing down on us always. This belief in our born-broken-ness, is always there no matter that we are not consciously aware of it. And it impacts on everything, I think. I think that I am not aware of how much it impacts, not even now. But to carry this image of our own grotesqueness into the world has to impact on how we present ourselves to others, on how much we are willing to risk, on the value we place on ourselves.

The good news is that this belief is just that – a belief. And it's a false belief. We're no more broken than anyone else. We're not perfect, for sure, but averagely flawed like other people. Not grotesque and horrific and monstrous. So, a false belief. And therefore a belief which can be changed by using EFT. Or, even without EFT, if you prefer not to use that, I invite you to use affirmations. 'I am well. I am whole. I am fine just as I am.' And repeat these as often as you can to reprogram your brain. (The EFT does work a lot more quickly and deeply though.)

Hugs,

Danu

A small observation on thoughts

Dear DONM …

A recurring theme of these letters is: 1) that our beliefs are programmed into our brains by our experiences and what we were taught; 2) therefore they create our feelings and thoughts; 3) our feelings and thoughts control what actions we take; and 4) the actions we take control our results and the quality of our lives.

I am forever banging on about how we can use EFT to change our beliefs and so have that cascade of effects work in our favour rather than against us.

But using EFT takes time, and it can be hard to remember to use it.

So here is a handy trick for other occasions. It's this:

You cannot help or control what thoughts come to you. They are born of your programmed beliefs.

But … you absolutely can control *the thoughts you have about those thoughts.*

You can have layers of thoughts, in other words. You can step a little bit aside from the programmed thought, and observe it and judge it and consider it.

And then you can decide what you will do next, whether you will believe the programmed thought or not, whether you'll act according to it or not.

So, if your automatic thought is something like, 'They'll all laugh at me if I do that', then you can consider that objectively.

Will they laugh at you? Will they really?

And then the answer will come from reality, and not your programmed beliefs.

The answer might be, 'No they won't.' In which case you can go ahead and do whatever that that belief was blocking.

Or, it could be that, 'Yes, they will.' Because not all programmed beliefs are wrong, of course. But then you can examine that thought too. And maybe ask yourself, 'Does it matter if they do? Maybe I could carry on regardless. Maybe

I don't care about their opinion – or not enough to stop me anyway.'

Or, you might decide, that, yes, it does matter that they will laugh at you, and therefore you won't do it. But that's okay. The purpose of this exercise is not to make you do things you don't want to. It's to let you examine thoughts and beliefs, and judge them, and make a clear conscious decision about them. It's about you choosing your actions from a place of clarity and consideration, rather than knee-jerk response. And in that is your power.

Hugs,

Danu

Is it really your job to fix everything?

Dear DONM ...

Another lie by the narcissistic mothers is that it's our job to fix things. This manifests as parentification when we are children – expecting us to take the parent's role so she can take the child's role. And so many of us grow up to be regular fixers, feeling responsible for everything.

As soon as we hear of our mother having any problems, we don our superhero cloak and off we go.

And so, we have a situation where, for example, if two of our siblings aren't talking to each other, we feel obliged to fly from one to the other, like the diplomatic corps, sorting it all out. Or if our mother has run out of her medication – totally through her own fault – it's us who has to drive all over town to try to source it for her.

This sense of responsibility, that it's our job to make sure everything works okay, is a real trap. And of course, it's not true. We are responsible for certain things for sure, but most of them are about our own life: our own children, our own house, our job. But we're not responsible for others' lives.

But yet, when we feel we are, that's the trap, isn't it?

We don't have the choice of whether to help solve the problem or not – we are obliged to. And that's exhausting.

The other problem with that is, with the games narcissists play, if we help out with a project, then we suddenly become responsible for the success of that project forever. So if our mother needed our help in finding a new house to buy, and ended up buying one that we found for her – well, any problems with the house, going forward forever, would be our fault. Conveniently forgotten would be the fact that we just gave her the information about it, and that she was the one who chose to buy it. No, the leaky plumbing and loud neighbours are our fault.

Or, maybe we did encourage her to buy it. Maybe that was part of what we had to fix. Maybe she was playing helpless, not able to make a decision, and so we did suggest she buy it, in all good faith of course.

And so, then it's definitely our fault.

It's a win for the narcissistic mother of course - she has you running around at the time of the purchase, and gains a stick to beat you with going forward.

The only way out of this trap is to stop feeling responsible for fixing everything. To decline the responsibility.

One way to do this is to stop responding to veiled hints that there's a job for you to fix. So if your mother says, 'Alex and Sheila aren't speaking', instead of responding that you'll speak to them both and sort it out, you say mildly and, above all, in a non-committal tone, 'Oh dear, I'm sorry to hear that.'

If she then becomes more direct and says, 'Would you have a word with them? You're so good at getting them to see sense.' you can answer something like, 'Ah, they're adults, they can sort out their own issues.'

If she insists, maybe laying on the guilt, 'But it upsets me so much to see them fighting' (trying to get you to be a Flying Monkey), you can respond with sympathy, 'Yes, I'm sure it does. That's hard for you, I have no doubt.'

It might seem hard to just let her keep her upset rather than try to solve it, but another, overlapping, lie is that we're responsible for her happiness.

We'll be discussing this more. For now just know that if she's unhappy about anything, well, she's responsible for her feelings, not you. You can empathise about her upset, but *you don't have to take it away*.

If the thing you're expected to fix is something urgent like her medication, you might make the choice of getting it for her this time as it's a safety issue, but stressing to her that you will not do this again. That she needs to plan ahead to make sure she doesn't run out, and if she doesn't do that, she will be responsible for that. Or putting a system in place that ensures she gets it automatically, to avoid both the drama games and your drop-everything-else involvement.

I know that's difficult, but if she is playing these games, then it's her taking chances with her health, not you. (Of course, you always have the choice to play her game in this example. None of this is about taking away your choices, but to hopefully make you see that you do have different options on how to respond.)

If she asks you straight out to fix something, you might like to cultivate the habit of saying, 'I'll think about that and get back to you.' That gives you space to consider it properly in your own time, without the spell that these narcissistic mothers can cast. None of this is to say that you can't help, or shouldn't help. It's that you could not feel automatically obliged to help, nor feel guilty if you do not.

She won't like you applying that boundary, of course. She might try to insist that you answer her now. One way to solve this is to say, 'If you insist on an answer now, the answer will be no.'

And if she does insist, then do tell her no, and keep to that decision. That way, you teach her that you mean what you say, and in that lies your power when she realises she cannot bully you as she used to.

And then, in your own space and time think calmly about the request, and decide if it's appropriate for you to do.

As ever, this feeling about it being your job to fix things is deeply engrained, and as ever I offer you the tool of EFT to erase it.

Hugs,

Danu

Is it really your job to make her happy?

Dear DONM …

We spoke of how it's our job (so we're taught) to fix everything. The carrot for doing that well is our mother's approval (always temporary and conditional); the stick is her unhappiness. And that feeds right into another belief we were fed: the belief that we are responsible for her happiness, or lack thereof.

And like the other lies she taught us, we believed it totally and in many cases are still living by it. This is why it's so easy for her to make us feel guilty for lots of things – because if the right thing is to make her happy, then obviously if we are not making her happy, we're wrong – and the guilt is for doing wrong. (The thing is that, as I often say, this guilt is *real* for sure, but it is not *true*. It is not justified.)

We are talking about a belief that we have to do whatever it takes, no matter the price to us, to keep her happy.

We are talking about the belief that if she has a problem, no matter the source of it, it is our responsibility to solve it. Even if she is the source of the problem through her actions, we must (according to this narrative) protect her from the consequences of her own actions and solve the problem. (Or, if the problem is not solvable, at least pander to her upset about the problem, operate the work-arounds the problem demands, and so on.) An example of this might be that if she has ill-health because she won't follow doctors' advice, we have to run around getting her special foods or painkillers at a moment's notice, and/or spend hours listening to her complaining about the ill-health.

We're talking about the fact that her merest wants take precedence over our own wants, or even our needs.

An example of that might be that she wants to be present in the labour ward when we give birth, and we allow it even though we really don't want her there at the time. Because if we say no, she would be unhappy, and we are responsible for her happiness.

This belief can even lead us to put her happiness above our

children's needs. Their birthday parties being spoiled because she wanted to be at them, and of course then made them all about her, for example.

The thing is that like so much else, this belief is a lie. One of her many lies.

The fact is that we are not responsible for our mother's well-being and happiness. We are not responsible for the well-being and happiness of any other adult except perhaps a spouse (and even then, that responsibility is limited). Yes, we are responsible for our own behaviour, and it is not right to proactively do wrong things to others. But that is not what we're talking about here.

We are not responsible to make her happy or keep her happy. If we make decisions that are in our best interests, it does not matter that they make her unhappy − again, with the only proviso that we do not do anything proactively unethical to her. So of course I'm not talking about it making you happy to hit her! I'm talking about decisions you make about your own life.

This motto is so true: 'If one of us has to be unhappy, it doesn't have to be me.' And you, no doubt are unhappy with many of the hoops you have to jump through to keep her happy.

The solution lies in letting go of the belief that it's your responsibility to make and keep her happy. There is huge freedom in that. You can start making decisions in your own best interests, and if she is unhappy, so be it. It is not that you will take pleasure in her unhappiness, but rather that you will be able to witness it calmly, knowing that it is her responsibility to make and keep herself happy, and if she is failing in that responsibility to herself, it is not your problem.

Let me repeat that: It is not your problem.

Now, she'll try to make it your problem. Be in no doubt about that. She'll rage, or weep, or cajole or try to manipulate, or send Flying Monkeys − or a combination of these.

But it's still not your problem, and the more you can know that deep down, the freer you are. You can calmly observe the rage, the tears, the sulks and so on, without falling for them.

In that, lies your freedom and your power.

So, how to get to that place where you no longer believe it's your job to keep her happy?

As we have been discussing, you can examine that belief when it pops up. Or you can keep telling yourself that it's not your job to keep her happy, and repeat it like an affirmation. Or fake it till you make it: ask yourself, 'What would I do in this moment if it was not my job to keep her happy?' And then do that, and ignore the churning stomach and thudding heart.

Or, as ever, I offer you EFT. That will help you delete and erase that programmed belief, so that you don't have to fake it – it will be real.

However you do it, it is so worthwhile to free yourself from the belief that you're responsible for her happiness. That, then, frees you to be responsible for your own happiness, which is as it should be.

Hugs,

Danu

All about power

Dear DONM …

Power. It's a loaded word, isn't it?

You may well have had a gut reaction when you read it, even.

I think that as DONMs we're often scared of our own power.

Our experience of power is that it's something to be abused. Something to be used for bad. To injure people rather than help them and support them.

No wonder we're scared of it. It seems like a monstrous thing, an out-of-control thing. A very dangerous thing.

And, so, in turn, no wonder we can be prone to avoiding it. To prefer to remain safely, as we see it, in our powerlessness.

Now, when I say 'as we see it', I mean of course, as our subconscious sees it. This isn't a rational or considered decision.

But it's no less real, and no less binding on us for that.

I think there are two possible fears (again, they're not articulated, so they are formless and imprecise).

The first is this: maybe we fear that we might become a nasty abusive person ourselves, if we had access to that power. This makes sense because we have never experienced power used for good, but only abused. So it feels at a deep level that the only thing that keeps us decent and kind is that we have no other options, that inside us is an abusive monster, needing only the right weapon, in the form of power, to burst forth from us like the creature in the movie *Alien*. And of course we like being decent and kind and all those good things. Of course we don't want to be like our narcissistic abuser.

And so we avoid that risk at all costs – and it *is* at all costs, pretty much, as remaining powerless leaves us powerless by definition. It leaves us weak and vulnerable. It leaves us ineffective in the world. Which, again, is a situation we don't want – but it's better (goes the subconscious's argument) than the alternative.

The other fear, which I suspect runs parallel with the first one (so it's not an either/or, it's both), is that, even if there is no monster/abuser lurking in waiting, that power is inherently too dangerous. That it's too big for us to handle. That it'll run amok all by itself, regardless of our good intentions.

When I think of this concept I always imagine myself being suddenly put in charge of say an F14 jet plane. Think of all that power – certainly too much power for my levels of competence and skill. Think of the death and destruction I would unwittingly cause through trying to harness that much power.

It is terrifying to consider, isn't it? I shudder at the thought. Much much better, and safer for everyone, and more sensible, for me to avoid being in charge of an F14.

And so, we can apply the same logic to the concept of power. We can consider that we would be too incompetent at being in control of power itself, and that it is much better, and safer, and more sensible, to avoid all power.

See if you can use EFT to work on this topic if it's an issue for you. When you visualise yourself being powerful, what image comes up? I used to visualise myself as a giant walking past houses only as tall as my knee, and as I walked through the town I wreaked destruction without meaning to, knocking over the houses, through the clumsiness of my sheer size. I tapped on that image and slowly it faded until now when I think of myself as being powerful I just feel ordinary sized, but strong, and I don't see myself causing any damage. In this way I can safely access my power. So you might find this exercise useful.

Or, as ever the option remains to look at this topic without EFT, and simply affirm and journal and so on, about your relationship with power. It's worth resolving one way or another. We are no use to anyone: not ourselves, nor anyone else, if we are powerless.

Hugs,

Danu

Victory over your narcissistic mother

Dear DONM …

One of the most horrendous aspects to the narcissistic abuse is that our narcissistic mothers teach us to abuse ourselves. In a very real way we take over her job for her. We don't do this consciously of course, nor deliberately. But the result is the same: we abuse ourselves just as she abused us.

We do this in various ways. For example by speaking as abusively to ourselves as she did. Perhaps out loud; more likely – and more insidiously and hence dangerously – quietly, in the very privacy of our own heads in abusive self-talk.

Every time you think, 'You're so stupid', or 'You'll never be good enough', or 'They won't like you', or 'You're mad to think you'll succeed at that', or 'You're so fat', or 'You're so clumsy', or 'You never do anything right', you're doing her abuse for her.

It also manifests in our behaviours. Every time you over-eat, or under-eat, or drink too much, or smoke, or don't bother to clean yourself or your home, you are continuing the abuse.

Every time you don't celebrate your successes, you are continuing her abuse.

Every time you don't give yourself time or space to mourn your losses and honour those appropriately, you are continuing her abuse for her.

It's like the abuse is a baton, and she passed it to you, and you took it and carried it forth.

Victory, therefore, lies in changing that pattern.

It's not easy, I know that. Because when I say 'you', I mean me too. I'm not immune from this. They say we teach what we need to learn, and I'm on this journey too. I'm writing what I need to hear as well.

And so, for us all, victory lies in changing the pattern. In treating ourselves well. In speaking to ourselves kindly. In feeding ourselves well. In meeting our needs and even our appropriate wants.

This is not just good because it's right for us. It's good because it's victory over that nasty woman. The only victory we'll get. We won't get an apology from her. We won't get recompense. We won't get acknowledgement from her, or from anyone else most likely.

But victory is possible. Beating her is possible. Winning this battle is possible.

And so, if it feels hard to do the right thing for ourselves for our own sake, maybe do it as a gesture of defiance to her.

Every time we make the higher decision, the self-care decision, we can think with satisfaction: *'You didn't win, you [fill in expletive of choice here]. You didn't defeat me. I am winning with every good decision I make.'*

And there can be satisfaction in that.

Hugs,

Danu

The curse of politeness

Dear DONM ...

I've written before about how normal rules don't apply with narcissists, in other words that we don't have to obey etiquette rules such as sending a thank you note for a gift. I'd like to explore this further, as the concept has been rearing its head for me recently.

A few days ago I was reading comments on a blog post and the commenter said that he and his wife teach self-defence for women, and what they find is the easy bit is teaching the defensive moves. What they find difficult is getting women to use their voices loudly.

And then I was speaking only last night to someone who teaches self-defence and he has the same problem: that one of the biggest things he has to teach is a politeness bypass. I love that phrase: *politeness bypass*.

And it reminds me how, many years ago, I worked for a group setting up a 'Stay Safe' programme for schoolchildren, which aimed to teach them to protect themselves against possible paedophiles. One of the steps was to yell 'NO!'. Not just say it, not even to say it firmly, but to yell it.

These things all have in common that they are counter to the normal rules of society which is that we must be polite and agreeable. Women, especially, are taught from birth to be polite and agreeable. And then we DONMs are taught it even more, not just to be polite and agreeable, but to be biddable and docile.

There are good reasons to be polite and agreeable. We humans are a cooperative species. That's how we came to rule the planet. All our wonderful intelligence and opposable thumbs would be little or no use to any one of us on our own.

But unconditional politeness is a trap, in my opinion.

Politeness is a contract. It acknowledges that we're both (i.e. me and the person I'm engaging in the politeness with) members of a cooperative species, and here we are manifesting that co-operation. When it works, it works well. But it needs both parties to be polite for it to work as intended.

What we need to learn, and learn well and powerfully, is that it's equally important to *not* be polite when that is appropriate. If the other person breaks the politeness contract, we are under *no* obligation to keep to it further. I think we need to learn this as women as well as DONMs. And we need to learn it as mothers, too, as we do our children no favours if we teach them that politeness is an absolute.

Inappropriate politeness leaves us weak and vulnerable.

Appropriate 'rudeness' gives us strength.

And by rudeness I don't mean proactive rudeness, which is why I put the word in quotes. I don't think there's ever a place for proactive rudeness. But it's definitely okay to answer rudeness with lack-of-politeness, and if society construes that as rudeness, so be it.

So, for example, if somebody gropes you on a crowded train, it would be appropriate to state loudly, 'You need to take your hand off me, NOW.' Yes, society doesn't like that, or permit it. But that rule by society allows people to grope us with impunity.

If someone knocks on your door looking for you to listen to their pitch, they are hijacking your time. They are being rude first. You don't have to be polite by standing there for ages listening to them when you're not interested in what they're selling. You don't have to be nasty, but in my opinion it's okay to be firm: 'I have no interest in this topic, so I'm going to go now. Goodbye.' – and then close the door.

The bad guys depend on our politeness. They use it against us. And that's whether it's 'mild' baddies such as salesmen at the front door, or extremely bad ones, such as predators.

And our defence is to give ourselves permission to stop being polite when that's needed.

We'll talk more about this, including coming up with a strategy on how to implement this.

Hugs,

Danu

It mightn't win you an Oscar, but ...

Dear DONM …

We've spoken about how sometimes you need a politeness bypass.

Now, this is often easier said than done. As we said, as women we're trained by society to be polite and biddable, and, as DONMs, doubly-so. So being appropriately impolite (aka assertive) can be difficult to do, and can feel very strange and even threatening.

The first thing to know is that when we're stressed, our body and our mind struggles to think calmly and strategically. When that happens it reverts to what it knows. And what it knows is politeness and acquiescence. Those are the default positions, so at a time of stress we automatically are polite and acquiescent. Which is often the exact opposite of what's needed under the circumstances.

So, the time to practise the new skills is when we are *not* under stress.

So what I suggest to you is that you quite literally rehearse these assertive moves. Rehearsing teaches your body to do it, so it'll be easy to use when needed.

Rehearsal is an amazing tool.

There's a reason sports-people and actors rehearse so diligently. It literally teaches your body what to do.

So, practise the skills, I suggest. Practise being assertive with door canvassers by opening a door, for example, and saying, 'No thank you, I'm not interested. Goodbye,' and closing it again. (Use an internal door rather than the front door if you don't want the neighbours thinking you've lost it entirely!)

Practise how you'll react to your narcissistic mother, depending on what you've decided is your preferred action. Say you've gone No Contact and want to practise ignoring her if she's trying to get you to talk to her. Well then, if possible get somebody to act as her, imploring you to speak to her, or demanding, or whatever (try a few variations), as you sweep by. Or, if you think your best bet would be to say,

'I've nothing to say to you. Go away,' then practise that.

If you're still in touch with her, practise setting the boundaries you want to set. Again if you can get someone to role-play her part, that'd be really good.

If you can't get a co-actor, just imagine her.

This will all no doubt feel very silly: telling the air that you won't speak to it, for example. But it's a real process for a real reason. Actors often act without props, just imagining them, too.

Practise using your voice, saying, 'No, I won't do that' and similar boundary-setting phrases. Practise saying them loudly and sternly. You don't have to say them loudly and sternly in real life (although you might, if the occasion demands), but if you're able to say them loudly and sternly, then it's simple to ease back on that and say it more quietly. This is just to get your body used to saying these things.

It's no use knowing in theory that you can be assertive, and impolite. You have to own that behaviour, and have it available to you, and rehearsal is absolutely the way to do it.

Hugs,

Danu

The grind

Dear DONM …

People often write to me to ask me is healing from this upbringing possible. I do believe that major recovery is possible, or I wouldn't be creating and sharing tools to help that recovery. We are so lucky to live in a time when resources like EFT exist. Nowadays recovery is far easier than at any time ever. We are also lucky to live in the age of the internet which means we can learn about resources such as EFT and others such as EMDR, and also learn about Narcissistic Personality Disorder to even know what was done to us.

However, it's also true that there is a lot of damage that has been done, damage that sometimes is hard even to quantify. What saddens me is the limitations that we're not even aware of, that confine us and squash us and make us tiny. The way we tell ourselves we cannot succeed, and think it's for real reasons – but it's because we were never taught success was allowed. Or maybe even expressly taught that success was not allowed for us. The way we think we're not deserving of love and think that's for real reasons, real flaws in us – not realising that was part of the lies too.

That's one of the many things I love about EFT, that it brings those hidden beliefs to light. All you have to do is to tap for the circumstance that you don't like, e.g. not being able to find a partner. And in tapping, up will come the belief around that, and you can tap for that, and so on, until the truth is revealed, and it's always a healthier and more powerful truth than you first realised.

I've spoken of this before. But what I want to say today though is how much I resent this. I resent having to put so much time into fixing what my narcissistic mother and narcissism-enabling father broke. Into healing what they injured. Into trying to get myself sorted enough to do what others take for granted. I'm tired of doing EFT! Yes, it's great, and I'm delighted to have it, but I'm so resentful of the necessity. It's so unfair that we DONMs have to work so hard to even get from a minus to even a zero, to work so hard on healing all the stuff before we can start to achieve.

What really annoys me about this whole DONM thing is the sheer waste of it all. All those days and months and years we could have been doing worthwhile and fun stuff, and instead we spent it in a combination of pandering to her, and in dealing with the fallout of our upbringing.

And even now, still dealing with the fallout, and for many of us, still pandering to her. The adventures we could have had, the career successes, the successful relationships, the rich friendships … and we either don't have them, or have to work so incredibly hard for them.

I've seen ads, along the way, for sporting excellence, and the ones I recall have a theme of the athlete grinding away, putting the hours in when it's dark and cold and there's no glory or company or comfort. Doing what it takes so when they get onto the pitch they're fit and in peak condition. I think of us DONMs when I see those, as we have to do the metaphorical equivalent of this training, but not even to excel as the sportspeople do, merely to cope, to be average in the world.

So, yes, I think we can recover, but I'm not sure we'll ever recover fully. Who knows what our full height would have been. And even that recovery comes at a high price of effort and determination and grind.

It's not fair.

Sorry to end on such a downbeat note. But it's not fair, and I do feel that, and sometimes it's good to acknowledge that too.

Hugs,

Danu

A suggestion for you

Dear DONM …

I spoke just now of the grind – the work to heal ourselves, and how it's such a waste of time in ways, and so unfair that it's necessary.

But given the reality that it is necessary if we want to heal, I want to share with you a very powerful exercise.

It's very simple for something so powerful. Here's what you do:

Stand in front of a mirror and *look at yourself full in the eyes*, and tap the EFT points in turn.

That's it.

But this one exercise is surprisingly difficult to do, and also amazingly powerful.

You will most likely struggle to meet your own eyes. It'll feel uncomfortable and wrong. It can feel very emotional, even overwhelmingly so.

The tapping will add to the intensity of the experience too.

You may well cry.

That's okay. There's a well of suppressed tears within us all, I think, and it's healing to have them come out.

You may find that you can't hold your own gaze for very long at all - that's okay too. Do what you can, and you can increase the length the next time. This is you truly seeing you, and honouring you and being with yourself, and that's a big step.

So, only hold your own gaze for as long as you can. If you cry, though, do keep tapping until the tears ease and dry up, and the upset is gone. The tapping will process the emotions which cause the tears, and move them on, and it's important to do that rather than let the emotions just hang around, or even worse, get repressed again.

If you could do this every day, for even 3 – 5 minutes, you would find it very healing. You will learn to be with yourself, to know yourself, to acknowledge yourself, to fully see yourself. This is powerful because, as part of the narcissistic upbringing, we were never allowed to fully acknowledge ourselves. Our narcissistic mother wanted all the attention on her of course, so we had to be outward-focussing towards her, rather than inward-focussing on ourselves. This exercise is to counterbalance that.

Also, given the toxic shame and the sense of being born broken that we have spoken of before, it's a huge step , and so healing, to just accept ourselves fully and unconditionally.

Hugs,

Danu

Be selfish!

Dear DONM …

One of the things that the narcissistic mothers teach us is that only *her* feelings matter. Our feelings are to be discounted by her and/or used against us as proof of our failure and faults. And we're taught to discount those feelings ourselves.

And only *her* desires matter. Ours are to be ignored by both her and us, or used as weapons against us because the more we want something the more she can hurt us by denying it or breaking it or taking it away.

And so we learn, growing up, to discount all that is important to us. To put ourselves last, if at all.

This is exacerbated and made worse by society's messages to women about being selfless givers. So we're hearing that message in the very air we breathe. It seeps into our pores and fills our lungs and we absorb that belief until it's very much part of us.

Also, we can hate and loathe so much what our narcissistic mother is, that we want to do the opposite of her in everything we can. So if she is selfish, we'll be unselfish.

And so, it might have been hard to read the title of this chapter: 'Be selfish'. Did it trigger stress for you? I wouldn't be surprised if it did, as it is so challenging to the rules we were taught to live by.

But this DONM journey is one of examining our beliefs, isn't it? Holding them up to the light and seeing if they're true or just part of the dysfunction.

And I offer you the possibility of looking again at this belief.

I offer you the suggestion that it's okay to be selfish. Indeed, even more radically: that it's *essential* to be selfish.

Being selfish gets a bad press, but I'd like us to reclaim that word.

I'm not talking about being self-centred or self-absorbed or anything like that.

Instead, I am speaking of being *appropriately selfish*. You don't leave your child hungry because you're too busy with your hobby to cook dinner. That's narcissistically selfish and of course we're not talking about that. But we DONMs can tend to be so far to the other end of that spectrum that we're falling off the edge.

For all the reasons shared above, we can often stop looking after ourselves enough. We fail to be appropriately selfish.

And that's what I offer you here – the prospect, the possibility of coming back to balance, of being appropriately selfish. Of taking time in the day to do something fun for you, of spending some money on you, of saying no to things that don't serve you.

It's part of putting good boundaries in place, in a way. You can't put in place good boundaries unless you know you deserve to. Unless you are selfish enough to, to phrase it another way.

If it feels too difficult to be selfish, if every part of you clenches in stress at the thought – then that is because she taught you well to put yourself last. As ever I recommend EFT to shift that basic belief.

All best for now, and keep going on your wonderful healing journey!

Hugs,

Danu

Can you go No Contact with her approval?

Dear DONM …

I've had many DONMs write to me and ask me when is it okay to go No Contact and have their narcissistic mother realise that it's justified. What horrible deed of the narcissistic mother is enough that even she (the narcissistic mother herself) will realise and accept their daughter's departure after that, and not blame her for leaving?

Well of course I don't know every narcissistic mother. But I would hazard a guess and say the answer is 'Never'. One of the defining traits of a narcissist, don't forget, is that they never are wrong. And I mean 'never', literally. Not 'rarely'. But *never*.

Hell could be an ice-block and pigs could be free-wheeling merrily over our heads, and a narcissistic mother would still be pouting or shouting or weeping that she DIDN'T do it and you're mis-remembering due to your vivid imagination, and it wasn't her fault anyway because you made her do it and you're over-sensitive to be getting upset about it and you're so mean to be so nasty to her when she's just a poor little old lady/ has a bad cold/insert drama of choice here.

So, she won't ever acknowledge that you're justified in cutting off contact. But you know, that doesn't matter. Or, more accurately, it only matters to the extent that we let it matter.

No, we won't be able to leave with her blessing and her acceptance and her understanding.

But it is us who puts that condition on it (for good and understandable reasons, don't get me wrong), and we can remove that condition if we choose.

Okay, that condition might well be ingrained and tough to remove (cough *EFT* cough!), but it is still a rule that we have somehow come to believe, and we can change it and remove it.

And in that lies our freedom. Yes, if we cut off contact she'll have her narrative about that and will rant or weep (depending on what she thinks will get most traction in that moment) to whoever will listen about her ungrateful daughter, or her delusional daughter, or whatever story she's telling.

You can't prevent that. There's no mileage in even trying.

But you can stop it preventing you from making the right choices for you.

You can free yourself from the need for her approval. You won't get it, ever (except temporarily and conditionally, as bait and manipulation), and freedom lies in accepting that fact and not trying any longer. And if it's right for you to go No Contact, then you can take that decision for you.

Hugs,

Danu

Narcissists' no-win situations

Dear DONM …

Narcissists, especially those towards the more malignant end of the spectrum, can delight in creating no-win situations to tie us up in knots. No matter what we do, we're in the wrong, and they manage to get drama out of it.

So, for example, they might want to organise a trip to the movies. So they check what's on and say, 'Would you prefer Film A or Film B?'

You say, 'Film A, please.'

And then you get a whole discussion, designed to wear you down, about how Film B is actually much better, and got better reviews etc., etc., until you agree to see Film B.

BUT …!

If you had said Film B, then most likely the reverse would have happened. Suddenly Film A is the best film ever and is the unmissable one.

We can never know for a fact if that would happen as we can't go back in time to test both options. But the fact that you never happen to pick the right film would be the clue.

So, you might get clever and say, 'Oh I don't mind. They both sound good. Let's go to whichever one you prefer.'

But no. That's too easy and too drama-free and too normal and sensible.

If you did that you would get, 'Oh I'm so sick and tired of this! I'm trying to organise a nice evening out for us and you won't even engage enough to show any interest in which film we go to. I'm tired of doing all the work here and making all the effort.'

Or you might get, 'God you're such a non-person aren't you, never having any opinions. No wonder everyone thinks you're so boring …', etc.

The script will no doubt change. But the underlying theme, that they'll manoeuvre things so that you're always in the wrong, remains.

Gotta love these narcissists, right? And by 'love' I do of course mean, hate, loathe, and despise.

Hugs,

Danu

Roots and wings

Dear DONM …

They say good parents give their children both roots and wings. Narcissists, of course, give their children neither.

I think of my own situation. I have no place I can really call my home town. In itself I don't mind that too much, as sometimes people do move house a lot, and that is not necessarily down to narcissistic abuse.

But what is down to the narcissistic dynamic is the fact that I have no roots to any family. We had no relationship with any aunts, uncles or cousins growing up. They all had relationships with each other, and we were the family left out in the cold, and I could never understand it. Now, of course I understand it fully. The result is when I grew into adulthood I didn't know anyone in my extended family. (In the last few years I have got in touch with a few cousins and that is wonderful. But those relationships are new and fragile as yet, until we get to know each other better.)

So there are no roots. I often feel unanchored. I have found my own home, with some success, but it never replaces that hole at the base of it all.

As for wings – hah!

When I look back on how woefully I was prepared for adult life, I am aghast. Between my parents and my educators, I was given no direction, no support, no encouragement. I launched into adult life clumsily and I was vulnerable. You don't know what you don't know, and it took me years to even figure out what the gaps were.

Rather than having roots and wings, children of narcissists are like tumbleweed.

Slowly I have realised the gaps, and equally slowly I have worked to fill them (education, financial management, self-care, etc.). But I am doing at 50 what most people do in their mid-twenties and those missing years will never be filled.

And I write this, not to whinge or complain, but because I

know this is the reality for us all. The details may differ between our different situations, but the broad picture remains the same: no one raised by a narcissist has either roots or wings. To provide these things requires mature and unselfish parenting, and that we definitely did not get.

I don't have any solution to offer; I'm still trying to figure it all out myself.

But I did want to acknowledge this reality for us all.

Hugs,

Danu

What about therapy with your mother?

Dear DONM …

As you know, daughters of narcissistic mothers expend hours and days and *years* of time, and infinite amounts of effort and energy, to fixing their relationship with their mothers. You have, no doubt, *been there, done that*.

This is because until we realise about Narcissistic Personality Disorder, *and* fully accept its implications, we either believe her lies that we're the problem, or even if we don't, we still cling to the hope the situation is fixable.

And I emphasise that knowing about Narcissistic Personality Disorder isn't enough – you need to also *fully accept its implications*, which are that she will not change, that she does not want to improve things (except on her terms which means your complete surrender).

But allowing ourselves to fully acknowledge exactly what Narcissistic Personality Disorder means is very hard. I know that. And until you're able to take the step of full acceptance, you might well be still trying to fix your relationship with her.

And as part of that quest, you might suggest she comes to counselling with you.

Or, she might even be the one who suggests therapy, and that can give you hope, and make you think that yes, there is a chance this can be fixed.

However, therapy with a narcissistic mother never ends well. As I remember, the experience of every single member of the forum I ran who went to therapy/counselling with their mothers was a terrible one.

This is because most often, the narcissistic mother picked the therapist, or it was one she was going to already. This meant that the therapist was already on the narcissistic mother's side; especially so if it was her current therapist as that therapist had already heard whole sagas about what a bad daughter she had, how much trouble the daughter caused, how nothing pleased her, etc.

Also the situation is further compounded by the fact that the narcissistic mother on the one hand, and her daughter on the other, had very different agendas about going to therapy. The daughter would be entering into it in a spirit of genuine exploration, trying to fix the relationship, to come to a better understanding, etc. The mother would be doing it in order to get the therapist to fix the daughter so she'd be more amenable and biddable.

So, in this scenario the mother and therapist would gang up on the daughter, and make her doubly convinced she was the problem, and a terrible person, etc.

I'm not saying that in this case the therapist would be deliberately ganging up on the daughter. (Although she might be; therapists can be narcissists too.) But therapists are only human, and they can be fooled by clever narcissists, and that's why it'd be happening.

I'll go as far as to say that if this is an on-going regular therapist of your mother's, then it's *guaranteed*, for reasons I explain below, that that therapist will have swallowed the Kool-Aid and will believe your mother's lies and that she (your mother) is the poor innocent victim.

No matter how innocent the intentions of the therapist, though, the result would be the same: you being abused further.

The other possibility is that you go to your therapist, who is forewarned about your mother's Narcissistic Personality Disorder (and I do sincerely hope that if you do have a therapist, she fully supports you and understands about Narcissistic Personality Disorder). Or it might be a therapist new to you both who is knowledgeable enough to identify your mother's narcissism.

And if the therapist does call your mother on her behaviour, what will happen then, *guaranteed*, is that your mother will find some way to stop going. She'll declare the therapist a quack who doesn't know what s/he's talking about, or declare that her going to therapy is a waste of time when it's *you* who's the problem, or suddenly come down with some illness that stops her going, or financial woes that mean she can't afford it (although that illness and those financial woes won't stop her doing other things).

And that is why, if your mother has an on-going therapist, that therapist is guaranteed to have been fooled by her, because the very fact that your mother is still going means that she's hearing only what she wants to hear from that therapist.

So, you'll see why therapy with your narcissistic mother isn't going to work as intended.

Having said all that, there can be reasons why you'd want to agree to therapy together. For example one very valid reason is that you want to know you have done absolutely all you can to sort out this relationship before you walk away.

If you do decide to do this, here are a few suggestions:

Make sure *you* pick the therapist, rather than letting your mother do it. Even better if it's your therapist to start with (although you may then be sure your mother will accuse that therapist of being on your side and ganging up on her, when the therapist calls her on any of her behaviour).

When you speak to the therapist beforehand, ask him/her what they know about Narcissistic Personality Disorder, and get them to tell you what they know rather than you asking direct questions.

You can say, 'I'm interested in coming to work with you with my mother. We're having issues that I believe involve Narcissistic Personality Disorder. Do you know much about that?'

And if they say, 'Yes, yes I do,' you can ask, 'Could you share with me some of your understandings about it?' and then let them speak.

Only pick a therapist who has accurate information about Narcissistic Personality Disorder. You'd be surprised and shocked at how many therapists do not know. And if they baulk at being asked questions like this, then they're not the therapist for you anyway.

And so, if you find a good therapist who does know about Narcissistic Personality Disorder, you and your mother can go there. The outcome will be that your mother throws some kind of hissy fit, storms out and refuses to go back – but you will have got the result of knowing you tried all that you could.

Hugs,

Danu

False doors and stone walls

Dear DONM …

One of the challenges of being a DONM is not only that you have to learn about Narcissistic Personality Disorder, but you also have to accept its implications fully; in other words, to accept the truth that your narcissistic mother never loved you, never *can* love you and never will love you. And that that's no reflection on your own worth whatsoever. It's about her being emotionally crippled so that she just doesn't have it in her to love anyone but herself.

As an aside, sometimes, from a safe distance, I can find myself feeling somewhat sorry for narcissists, who miss out on the joy of loving others. Love makes our world vibrant and full of colour, and here they are living in a kind of grey-sepia flat world without that.

But then I recall just how much devastation and hurt and misery they cause, and my sympathy dissolves.

But anyway.

Until we realise this truth about our mothers we can spend years and decades of our one precious life knocking on a door that will never ever open. It's not even a door, it's a solid wall painted to look like a door. Or, maybe even, a solid wall that doesn't even look much like a door (because sometimes narcissistic mothers don't even bother to pretend very hard), but our own understandable desire, and society's expectations of what a mother is, convince us it's a door.

But no matter how well or badly it's painted, it's not a door; it's solid rock. And solid rock can never swing open.

Freedom lies in accepting this fact, no matter how painful. You can use EFT by yourself to make those shifts, or just make the decision in some other way. By deciding to, maybe. This perhaps sounds flippant but it's not. Your freedom is just a thought away.

And once you've made the decision, then what?

There may well be grief as you process this (and EFT will

help with that too; just tap as you are feeling the grief). But after that, there is freedom.

And I invite you to see the possibilities in this. The fact is that the endless futile knocking on that stone wall took so much of your energy and attention. It was exhausting, wasn't it? And now you don't have to do that any more!

Think of all that you can do, and be, and have, once that energy is freed up! You have been working so very hard on a useless task, and now you can (after a rest) use that energy and power for your own purposes.

And you can redefine yourself too. You can find out who you really are now that you know you're not your mother's unlovable child. I repeat, you are *not* who she said you were. She held up a false mirror to you, to show you a grotesque caricature of yourself, because that kept you weak and trapped. But you are not who she said you were.

One small but effective step I recommend is to tap (i.e. use EFT) the affirmation 'I am not who she said I am', over and over for a few weeks until that shift happens and you know the truth of it. You don't have to spend hours doing it, but try to incorporate it into your life – five minutes three times a day perhaps. And when you're standing waiting for a kettle to boil, or hanging around at the front door waiting for someone to finally be ready to leave … in other words, in those spare moments we all have, tap each point in turn saying on each one: 'I am not who she said I am.'

This process is incredibly freeing and empowering as you will find.

Hugs,

Danu

'Are you *still* going on about that?'

Dear DONM ...

One trait of emotional abusers, including narcissists, is that they a) do not want to resolve anything, and b) don't want you to insist on them resolving anything. And so they operate a Magical Cosmic Reset Button which means that after a certain amount of time has passed, they don't have to discuss a previous problem or situation. The slate is wiped clean.

This of course means that they never have to acknowledge what they did, and more importantly, that they never have to change their behaviour in order to make sure they don't do the same thing again.

The only problem with this wonderful system is when you start trying to mess with it and hold them accountable. And their go-to line to stop you in that attempt is: 'Oh you're not *still* going on about that are you?'

The word 'still' means that you've been holding onto it far too long. You're bearing grudges. You never let things go, you. Never forgive and forget. You're so unreasonable.

Or, they might place the emphasis a bit differently and say: 'Oh you're not still going on about *that* are you?'

The word 'that' shows how trivial the incident was, and here you are blowing it up into a huge issue. It was a nothing, a moment, a minor thing, but no, you have to go on and on and *on* about it don't you? You have to make a federal case out of it. You're so unreasonable.

And, on the face of it, what they say sounds plausible. After all we know it's not adult or mature to bear grudges or to take offence at every tiny thing.

But you know, what they're saying is *not* plausible. Don't fall for it.

With regard to the length of time since the incident happened, the fact is that an incident is not resolved until it's resolved. Something like that is not a flesh-wound that heals itself with time. It's a tear in fabric that needs mending and will stay torn until that happens, and perhaps even fray more in the meantime.

It is *entirely* reasonable to have a conversation like: 'I didn't like the way x situation happened. Can we talk about it and find a solution going forward that meets both our needs?'

As for their second ploy, implying that the situation was trivial: my thoughts are that it doesn't matter if it's trivial (once you're not being pathologically controlling). If it's important to you, it's important in the relationship and should be open for discussion. In a healthy relationship, these things can be discussed with an open mind on both people's side, and a good solution or compromise found. Sometimes the solution is that they explain their position and you accept it once you realise their side of it, rather than them changing their behaviour.

So, say you ask a friend, 'I don't like it when you don't text to say you're safe once you've got home,' and they say, 'I hate feeling I have to text you. We've said our goodbyes and to me that's enough.' Well, the solution might be either that they text in future, or that you accept that they don't text when you realise how big a deal it is for them. In a way it doesn't matter what the actual solution is; the important thing is the respectful and caring discussion about it.

But my guess is that if you're psyching yourself up to bring up a topic with your narcissistic mother, it's not trivial at all. You let the trivial things go because they're not worth the trouble. These are big and important things to you. So don't fall into her trap of believing that because she deems it trivial, you have to let it go. As already said even if it was trivial, it'd be fair to discuss it, and it's *not* trivial anyway.

So don't believe her when she does whatever her preferred variation of 'Oh you're not still going on about that are you?'

Having said all this, though, the reality is that narcissists will never be held accountable for their actions, and will never agree to discuss it. If you try to insist, they'll block you another way. My own mother would snap, 'That's *enough*, Danu!' and that was usually enough to stop me cold. And on the rare occasions that it didn't work, when I, heart thudding and stomach churning, would persist in something important to me, she'd collapse in tears and deflect it that way.

So none of what I'm saying here is about finding a way to get through to your narcissistic mother and make her understand your position. There is no such way *to* find.

It's about your own awareness though. It's about you recognising that you are not holding grudges, or getting upset about trivial things, no matter how much she tries to spin it that way. It's about you seeing it for the manipulation it is, rather than believing her.

Hugs,

Danu

Giving yourself permission

Dear DONM ...

Our society is based on a hierarchical model where so many people get to be the boss of us. That was true when we were children for sure, from parents to teachers to even random adults. In a healthy model the reins of authority were handed over to us when we were old enough.

And even so, I think many people are still looking for authority to tell them something is okay to do. It seems to me that in their fear they're looking for somebody in charge to say: 'It's okay to start your own business/write your novel/go travelling around the world.'

How much so does this apply to DONMs who have experienced nothing but the misuse of authority?

I get a lot of emails from DONMs asking me, in effect, if it is okay to go No Contact with their narcissistic mothers. I understand that entirely – for years and years I kept in contact with my parents despite hating every minute of it and being emotionally bruised after every encounter, because I thought you had to. I didn't realise I was allowed to not be in touch with my parents. If I'd had anyone to ask for permission, I sure as hell would have done it too.

I make a point of course to never give permission as such as that's absolutely not my place. But I try to say that they can give themselves permission, that they're allowed to do that, that they're the boss of their own lives – and that's what I want to say to you too. And maybe to myself as well, as I need constant reminding!

So I have realised that one of the hugely empowering things in your life, with regards to your narcissistic mother and everything else – is to *give yourself permission*.

For example, no one gave me permission to set up the DONM website. I just did it. And any of you can do the same.

Also, I'm a novelist of sorts. When I had my first novel published a good few years ago, I was amazed the number of people who said, 'Do you not have to have a degree in English to write a novel?' In other words, did I not need permission/validation from authorities such as a university to do this? Nope. I just wrote it.

There's security in having permission, I think, that you don't have when you do stuff yourself. Someone else has said it's okay. But in so many things in life, there is no one who's authorised to say it's okay, so you could be waiting forever.

I'd like to offer you the possibility of considering this thought, and thinking what you might do in your life if you had sense of being allowed to do it. And then, giving yourself that sense. It might sound mad, but just try it: Speak it aloud. Say: 'I [your name] hereby give myself full and absolute permission to do x.' (I'm sure it goes without saying that this only applies to things that are ethical.)

Be aware of the sensations in your body as you say this. Do you feel a tension when you do? This shows that you don't really believe in your own permission. Which is fully understandable for all the reasons shared above.

If this is the case, you can just plough on regardless, ignoring the sensations, and when your body realises it's not dangerous to do this, it'll feel better. Or, use EFT to erase the fears and doubts.

When we follow our dreams, we fulfil our own lives and souls, but I think we also add to the world. As Marianne Williamson says in her book *A Return to Love*, when we play big we give others permission to do the same. So it's a win-win.

So go on: give yourself all the permission you need!

Hugs,

Danu

What does it mean?

Dear DONM …

One thing I've learned is that humans are meaning-creating creatures. This is how we see images in clouds, for example.

We don't just look at things and accept them. We instead ask what it means, and more, *decide* what it means. The problem with this is two-fold: the first is that we can very likely be wrong about what it means, and the second is that we do this so quickly and intuitively and subconsciously that we don't even realise we're doing it. And all that means that we never get to question these decisions or judge them to see if they're right.

So, if our mother is distant and abrupt and unloving when we're small, subconsciously we conclude that it's because we're unlovable (rather than the fact she is incapable of loving anyone.) And that becomes part of our map of our reality, and it impacts on us for our whole lives.

So one essential step on the road to healing is to look at the meanings we put on things. This is easier said than done as the meanings happen instantly. It takes vigilance to catch them and question them. And I'm far from good at this myself. I share it because I know it's so good to do, not because I'm expert at it. But any false meaning caught and deflected is better than none, so it's well worth the effort.

And so, if a friend doesn't return your call or text quickly, you might immediately conclude that she's cross with you. An equally valid interpretation (given you don't know the facts) is that she's busy, or her phone is out of charge.

I think we DONMs are too quick to assume the bad interpretation of everything. It's totally understandable of course, but it still doesn't do us any favours. So the more we can catch ourselves doing that, and stopping it, the better.

One good exercise is to write down the fact of what happened. For example: My friend didn't ring back.

And then add, 'Which means …' and freewrite what you think it means. 'She's cross with me'. And then add, 'which means ...' and freewrite that. You might end up with something like say, 'Which means she won't want to be friends with me any more.' Continue this process, applying the meaning to every stage: 'Which means that I will be friendless and that I'm impossible to get on with and no one wants to be friends with me.'

This isn't a fun exercise, I know. But it's just bringing up to the light the stuff that's going on anyway for you beneath your awareness. No wonder you feel so stressed and upset when she doesn't ring you back.

So then, when you're finished, look at your final disaster-thinking. You can use EFT on that statement if you wish to nullify it and make it lose its power, but even without that, look at it and realise how untrue it is. You have built the proverbial mountain out of the molehill. (Again, I do this too, all the time ...)

And recognising the games your brain is playing on you with all this can really help you to neutralise it. Because even if it's true that your friend is cross with you, it doesn't follow that she'll want to stop being friends with you. And even if that is true, it doesn't follow that no one ever wants to be friends with you.

And if, perhaps, that *is* true. Well, better to know it than not, and in this case you have identified the real problem and that is when you could perhaps look into therapy to find out why.

But I bet you'll find that your end-of-line disaster-thinking is so untrue as to be absurd and will help you realise that the meaning you put on things doesn't always serve you.

Hugs,

Danu

Helping your inner child

Dear DONM ...

When I was 12, I went through the ceremony of Confirmation in the religion I was raised in. I am sharing this with you, not because of the exact occasion, but because it was an occasion that was supposed to be about me. Because I thought that it would be a time that I'd be made a bit of a fuss of, be a bit special to them for once.

That morning, all was chaos as my mother was trying to organise us all. There were three children younger than me, including an 8-month old baby, so I can see the pressures. But my father was there, and my younger brother was 10, so surely able to help a bit.

My mother needed something from the shops about 15 minutes' walk away and she ordered me to go and get it. I recall the shock I felt. This was my special day! Surely I couldn't just be sent down the shops like it was an ordinary day. I didn't think of it till afterwards, but why couldn't my father or brother have gone? I did try to protest that I shouldn't have to go on this day of all days, and she yelled at me and I caved immediately as ever.

It wasn't that I objected to going to the shop or to helping out. But to be *ordered* to do so like this, with absolutely no mention or consideration that it was my special day really hurt. If she'd spoken to me gently and nicely, and said, 'Danu, I know it's your special day, and I'm so sorry to ask you but would you be able to go down to the shop for me?' then it would have been very different. But of course she didn't do that.

There was, as usual, no softness or gentleness or understanding. To add insult to injury, we only had one hairbrush for the whole household (which is bizarre in itself, as I think of it), and I couldn't find it, so had to go with my wild thick hair unbrushed and messy.

I can still recall 12 year old me walking to the shops, shoulders slumped, upset, confused, burning with the injustice of it, hurting at yet again realising that I didn't matter, I wasn't important to them at all, that they were just going through the motions of parenting – doing the confirmation thing because that was what you did. It certainly wasn't about me in any way.

But as I recalled this experience, I did something different. In my imagination, I, the Danu of today, stepped into the scene. I walked up to 12-year-old Danu and fell into step beside her.

'Hey,' I said to her.

She looked up in surprise at someone arriving beside her out of nowhere.

'I'm you in 40 years' time,' I told her. 'The grown-up you.'

She didn't freak out or run away or anything. This being my imagination and my story, she reacted as I needed her to: calmly, as if it was totally reasonable for a time-traveller from the future to come back to chat to her. She was instead curious and interested in what I had to say.

And what I had to say was this, 'Danu, you need to know that this is no reflection on you, or your value as a human being. Yes, the message is that you are so valueless that even your special days are nothing to them. But it's a wrong message. It's a false message. It's about a flaw in *them*, not in you.'

I spoke urgently, as this was essential information for her to know: 'You are a wonderful valuable human, just as everyone else is. You are *not* less-than. They are giving you false information. Yes, you have to endure the day as they create it, but you don't have to believe the subtext about your value. Okay?'

She brightened. Her shoulders straightened a bit and she stood taller. 'I understand,' she said. 'Thanks for that.'

And she walked off towards the shops and I stood and watched her go, happy that she felt better about it

*

Well, that's ridiculous, you might say. That was just all in your imagination. For sure. Of course it was. But the thing is that that the hurting 12-year-old Danu was only in my imagination too. The real 12-year-old Danu is long gone.

The scar and hurt are in the present, and live in my imagination and my mind, so I can do things in the present and in my imagination/mind to heal them. Now, when I think of that situation it doesn't hurt any more. I've re-written history. Okay, not real history. But history in the only place it exists – my mind. Now when I think of that day I see 12-year-old Danu being very aware of what's going on, and it helping her immeasurably.

Could you try this yourself for upsetting memories? (Using due caution of course, use your judgement on whether it's safe for you or not.) If it's a very bad memory that really cannot be perceived in any different way – e.g. abuse, well then you can tell her that it wasn't her fault, and that she/you do survive it. And you can be the loving adult helping her through it. If it's too triggering for you to be there while she's experiencing it, you can go to her after an incident. I'd love to hear how you get on with it.

There's a way of using EFT to help even more with this memory work, and I'll talk more about that next.

Hugs,

Danu

Using EFT with your inner child

Dear DONM …

I know that heading might feel very weird and new-agey. But you can think of your inner child as just the memories in your current brain, as we shared in the previous letter. And EFT is, well yeah it is a little bit new-agey, but it works for all that.

To use EFT for your memories, you go and visit the younger you in your memory, as I shared in the last letter. If it's a different younger you than you met before, introduce yourself to her again. She is, in some very real way, a different person from the previous memory.

And this time you tell her you have a way of making her feel better, and would it be okay with her if you tried it. (You always respect her boundaries like this.) If she says no, accept it fully, and ask her would she like you to stay and talk with her, or hold her hand, etc. Do whatever she's comfortable with.

You might find that after a while she asks you what your method of making her feel better is, once you're not pressuring her. But if she never does, so be it. Try it on another memory another time.

And when you find a younger you who is willing, what you do is this: if she is already upset about what happened, just sit beside her and visualise/imagine yourself tapping on her. Tap on all the points in order. Keep tapping just as if she were a real person until the stress leaves her and she's calm about it.

Or, ask her to tell you what happened, and tap on her while she tells you.

At the end you can offer her a better outcome. You can say, 'Instead of you being here in your room crying after what Mum said to you, would you like to go somewhere nice? We can go anywhere you like.'

If she says yes, then ask her where she'd like to go, emphasising she can go wherever her imagination chooses: a beach, a fairground, the moon – anywhere! And once she chooses, in your imagination bring her there and be with her for a while there. And when it's time for you to come back into the real world, ask her who she'd like to come and be with her there – a friend maybe, or an animal. And conjure up that image when she asks, and you can leave her there safely and happily.

You will find this exercise to be incredibly powerful and helpful for you, the you-of-today as of course it changes your memories too.

I do urge you not to dismiss this suggestion as being too weird, as it really is powerful for healing.

Hugs,

Danu

It's just smoke and mirrors and curtains

Dear DONM …

Do you remember that iconic scene in *The Wizard of Oz* where they pull back the curtain to reveal that the Emperor is just a pathetic little man operating levers?

That image comes to me often when I think of narcissistic mothers, because they are like that.

Assuming she does not have a financial hold over you (which is very possible; they're good at manipulating situations like that), and that she is not violent towards you (and if she is, please please know you don't have to accept that and have options there too), her power is all smoke and mirrors and curtains.

Her power is only words, in that case. And her words only have the impact we give them. It's totally understandable that we give them huge impact as we've been trained to do since birth, but what I am sharing with you now is the possibility that you break that pattern.

This goes back to boundaries that we spoke of before. Know that you have the power to put boundaries in place, and there's probably (depending on your specific situation) nothing she can do about that.

The example I share applies to my father rather than my mother. My mother never showed any interest in me (beyond a vague, 'How are things with you?' which she would interrupt as soon as whatever I said triggered some thought of her own) and so I never had to give any hostages to fortune with her. However, my father showed great interest in my life, and would ask about specifics. This might sound great but it used to make me so stressed when he did it, and it took me ages to figure out why.

I finally figured it out: he would ask questions about a situation until he could find, or assume, something bad about it, and then commiserate about that, having fully burst my bubble. I bet if I told him I won the national lottery he'd say mildly, 'Oh, well done. Do they send you a cheque?' and when I'd say,

'No, you have to go up to their headquarters to collect it,' he'd commiserate sadly, 'Oh that's awful, hard luck.'

So yes. Once I realised this I determined to never tell him anything important again. And once I had managed to pluck up my courage to actually follow through on my determination (and that took a while for sure), the next time he asked about a big project of mine I said, 'I don't want to talk about that project any more.' He said in the dangerous voice he used if he was being thwarted, 'And why don't you want to talk about it any more?'

I kept my voice calm even though my heart was racing, and said lightly, 'I don't want to talk about why I don't want to talk about it.'

His face was a picture! Fury for sure, but frustration too because he had lost. He realised we could go on endlessly, turtles all the way down, if he pursued it: 'I don't want to talk about why I don't want to talk about why I don't want to talk about it any more' and so on.

And that was the day I realised no one can make you be part of a conversation you don't want to be part of. The day I realised they don't get to be the deciders of what I have to share and discuss. It was very empowering and freeing, and I want to share that with you too.

Hugs,

Danu

How a cycling hint has helped me with life

Dear DONM …

I'm a keen cyclist. Not a very fit or hard-core cyclist, mind, but a keen one. And one thing I struggle with is hills. I read a hint on a cycling forum that when you're cycling up a difficult hill, to keep your eyes on the ground in front of you (as much as is compatible with safety of course, glancing ahead every so often to check). Keeping your gaze close rather than long, will help, they said.

Well, I tried it and it totally does help. They didn't know why, and I'm not sure either but I think it's because it breaks the task into tiny manageable bits. Instead of seeing the huge hard hill ahead of you, you are only focussing on this tiny bit of it.

And I think this is a good metaphor for life, whenever you reach metaphorical hills. And, let's face it, DONMs have more than our fair share of metaphorical hills don't we?

I think that when all is too difficult, just take baby steps. Do the tiniest little thing you are able to do. It doesn't even matter if it's the right thing. It is movement and when you're stuck, movement in any direction will give you much-needed momentum. So do the one tiny thing you can, focussing on the immediate surroundings (still metaphorically speaking).

If you look up and try to make a big picture plan, then it can be overwhelming and you don't know where to go and what to do and so you stay stuck. (Obviously if you're in a position to look at the big picture and make a strategic plan, then do that. This is advice for when that's not possible for you.)

And so, take baby steps, and keep taking baby steps for as long as you have to, until you are far enough away from the original blockage (I am mixing my metaphors dreadfully here, I know!), and can then look around you. And yes, you might be far from where you should be going, but you can go from the new place to the correct destination then, when you have more momentum and less panicked paralysis.

Hugs,

Danu

Sometimes it really is about you!

Dear DONM ...

I spoke before about how it's not narcissistic to want it to be about you. I know that can be hard for DONMs to realise because we were taught so hard that it is never ever, ever about us. But that is a message that has to be handed back I think. Because sometimes it really is about you.

This was brought home to me very strongly some time ago. A friend of mine was due to have her first baby. Now, we don't have the custom of baby showers where I live, so normally there is no official 'send off' to women in her situation.

But she wanted to acknowledge this special occasion so she organised a women's night, with chat and poems and dancing, and good wishes for her. I was so impressed with the way she did this, claiming her right to have this special occasion for herself, and arranging it accordingly.

Even more so, when, during the evening, we were dancing and she put herself in the middle of the circle, so that we were dancing around her. She was very clearly and deliberately making herself the centre of the whole evening.

And this is a woman who is in no way narcissistic, let me stress. She is kind and warm and gentle and compassionate and equally ready to make others' occasions be about them.

Which is why it was such a powerful lesson to me: You clearly don't have to be narcissistic to make it about you.

I think that many DONMs, including myself, have trouble with that concept as all we ever experienced was narcissistic attention-seeking.

So to see this woman, with such grace, make it *appropriately* about her, was so good for me to witness. I learned that it's okay to make it about me when it's appropriate. And I would love if you could learn this second-hand from her example.

Because, sometimes it really is about you.

It really is.

What things do you think are appropriately about you? Maybe you could make a list. In this way you are consciously naming and claiming these things. Here are some suggestions: Your birthday. Your wedding (that's about you and your spouse). Your graduation. Your baby shower. Your bereavement. Your miscarriage.

And, I suggest, you need have no shame about wanting to make those about you, about you being the centre of attention then. You need have no shame about ring-fencing or protecting those occasions from being hijacked by your mother.

Hugs,

Danu

When someone says they love you, it should feel like they do

Dear DONM …

Narcissistic mothers are, in my experience, very good at saying 'I love you.' But they don't act like they love us; far from it.

This is one of the many forms of the narcissistic abuse called *gaslighting*. Gaslighting refers to the way narcissists and other abusers re-write history in their favour, and lie to us about reality to the extent we doubt our own perceptions in the face of their insistence.

And because we are trained to believe her version of reality above our own, we can end up believing she loves us even though, truly, it doesn't feel like that.

Or, we begin to think that narcissistic abuse is what love really is, is what love feels like. Of course we do. How can we not, when it's our main, or only, experience? And of course this sets us up for future abuse as we accept the same behaviour from others who say they love us.

So they tell us they love us even as they demean us and intimidate us and dismiss us and invalidate us and gaslight us and undermine us and sabotage us … and we can still believe them.

It can take a long time to realise what love feels like, and even longer to insist upon it from those who say it.

These are my thoughts on what healthy love feels like.

It actually applies to all relationships I think. It applies to those who say (either implicitly or in as many words): 'I am your friend', too as much as those who say they love us.

Love feels respectful. It does, indeed, as St Paul is quoted as saying in the Bible, feel 'patient and kind'.

People who love you can disagree with you, and even criticise you, but will do so mostly in a respectful, patient and kind way. I say 'mostly' as anyone can be impatient and lose their temper once in a while, but it should very much be the exception and not the rule. And in healthy relationships they should apologise afterwards. And I think that even when healthy people lose their tempers, they still don't get abusive. They might yell, 'I am sick and tired of the way you do xyz,' but they don't yell abuse at you, telling you what a horrible person you are to do xyz.

You can relax knowing that you are safe. I think this is a good measure: check in with your feelings around this person – are you serene and calm and relaxed about being with them? Or is there a bit of tension and nervousness? Do you have to feel alert? This is a good indicator, as your feelings will not lie to you, even though your poor brain-washed brain might.

Those who truly love you encourage you and support you in your endeavours. They do not undermine you. This can be a subtle one as abusers can cleverly undermine while seeming to support you. 'Here, let me help you with that, you know you're not that good at it and I want you to succeed in it.'

Those who love you see the best image of you. They're not naïve about you: they see you clearly, faults and all. But they hold the full package in high esteem. They see more good about you than bad. (On the other hand, the abusers are all about your faults and have a very poor image of you, which they are happy to share regularly with you.)

Those who love you respect your boundaries.

And so, one lesson I have learned is to mark well how people treat me, and to assess our relationship based on that. Words are cheap. It is easy to say you love someone, but not so easy to act in love. The act, then, is the thing that has the value.

Words can even be weapons used against us, as manipulation. Sometimes abusers know they don't love us but they say it to reel us in, to manipulate us. Listening instead to the actions will protect against that too. And by actions I mean consistent actions. Narcissists can act well for a while, in the 'courtship' phase of a relationship. But they cannot keep it up for too long.

And what if the narcissist means it when they say I love you? I think my narcissistic mother genuinely believed she loved me, and she may even have had some feelings of mild fondness for me. But it was a cheap love, love that demanded nothing of her, no care or thought or kindness or empathy or even the tiniest sacrifice. That kind of love is no use at all. It is pure self-indulgence on her behalf, giving her the warm fuzzies of saying it and even feeling it. It is her love serving her, as everything serves a narcissist. I have no need of such love. I deserve better than that.

And so, of course, do you.

Hugs,

Danu

Feeling the feelings

Dear DONM …

One thing we DONMs have in common is that we were forbidden from expressing negative feelings. In many cases we were even forbidden from feeling them. In time we hide them, even from ourselves perhaps, and certainly from the world.

I remember my mother coming home one day, all proud, because a local shopkeeper had told her, 'Oh I love to see Danu coming in. She's always so bright and cheerful that she cheers up the whole place.'

And for sure, that's what I was like. And now, if ever I was to speak with my mother about my youth she'd say, 'But you were happy! You were bright and cheerful and chatty.'

And that is true. Well, the bit about bright and cheerful and chatty is true. The bit about being happy? Who knows. My relationship with my own emotions was so perverted that I don't even know. I know I had depression and suicide ideation (and one genuine attempt age 16) and eating disorders going on. In later years, still cheerful and outgoing and chatty, I had addictions which I have battled until recently.

And I didn't dare express anything else. 'Stop crying or I'll give you something to cry about', was a favourite statement in my house whenever I was upset. (Particularly when I was upset about her treatment of me; I was allowed to be upset about other things in fairness.) You might have heard phrases like, 'Turn that frown upside down', or 'Smile!'.

And so we DONMs ended up not even knowing what we were feeling half the time. And maybe being so repressed we didn't feel anything at all the rest of the time. It's impossible to clamp down on bad emotions without also clamping down on good ones.

Our narcissistic mother's theft of our emotions is one of her worst crimes in my opinion. Emotions are our barometers for our lives. They're an absolutely integral part of our birthright as humans.

And so I think one of the most essential steps on this journey is to reclaim our emotions. And that isn't as easy as it sounds. We're so trained to ignore them that half the time we don't even 'hear' them. We're not even aware of them. Or we're eating them or drinking them or smoking them or purging them or injecting them as ways of avoiding them.

Emotions can be scary. They can be overwhelming. No wonder we don't want to risk that. Here's the thing though – emotions cannot harm us. Even the worst sadness or grief, cannot harm us. It does feel uncomfortable, but that feeling is just another emotion. And remember, emotions are something you *have*, not something you *are*. All emotions are temporary.

I've mentioned it before but the trick of observing your emotions while they're happening is a very powerful one. Let part of you be a little bit aside from it, narrating it to yourself almost like a sports commentator. 'The pain is in my chest, it feels like a stone, it hurts, so much grief', helps you keep an anchor in the calm world so you don't feel like you're drowning in the emotions.

And of course I find EFT to be wonderful to use during such times. Just tap on each statement: 'the pain in my chest, feels like a stone', etc. EFT doesn't push down the emotions; it helps process them and move them on, so it's a healthy way to deal with them.

I remember one time spending maybe an hour, maybe more, sobbing and bawling and tapping as I processed the grief around: 'Who I am is not acceptable' – which is the message I was taught all my life, and I know you were too.

Because that's the thing. Emotions need to be felt. They're messengers to us, and they have to be heard and then let go. None of this is about wallowing in emotions – that is equally unhealthy. But we are under no obligation any more to bury them as our mother wanted us to.

What if you can't feel emotions at all? What if they're so repressed they feel out of reach entirely?

You can try a few things. One would be to tap on the statement: 'It's safe to feel my emotions.' Or, conversely, if it sits better, 'It's not safe to feel my emotions', and release that belief. (EFT works for both positive affirmations and for erasing the current disempowering situation.)

You can try freewriting instead of, or as well as, EFT.

Also, try to remember during the day (either by yourself, or set alarms on your phone perhaps), to scan your body and your awareness to see how you're feeling in that moment. Feelings are held in the body, usually in a column from high in your throat down to your solar plexus. That's why emotions are called *feelings*, because we *feel* them. When you do this scan, just be aware of the feelings – you don't even have to label them for this exercise, although if you can, that's even better.

Also, check in on the following (non-exhaustive) list of emotions and ask yourself, 'Do I feel this right now?' Do this when things are peaceful enough, rather than in the middle of a crisis. A crisis is no time to practise new skills.

Here is the list of emotions:

- Love
- Fear
- Surprise
- Joy
- Hurt
- Anger
- Disappointment
- Sadness
- Shame
- Disgust
- Anticipation
- Interest
- Anxiety.

As you become used to feeling your emotions, you might end up feeling very negatively towards your mother, and that might trigger your desire to shut down as you're doing something so forbidden (i.e. thinking badly of her, which was the ultimate crime of course).

If possible, allow yourself to feel the feelings. They are very justified. They were a long time coming. Your negative emotions about her will not hurt her directly (and of course I do not recommend lashing out at her), nor will she know about them by some kind of magic. I know it probably felt like that when you were small, but you are adult now and she has no special powers.

Once you get used to feeling your emotions, the next step is to know how to safely express them, and we'll talk about that next.

Hugs,

Danu

How to express your emotions safely

Dear DONM ...

We spoke about getting in touch with your feelings, and now we are going to discuss how to express those feelings.

These are my thoughts on the issue; as ever, take what you find useful and leave the rest.

I think it's important to make sure not to express your feelings in a damaging way, in a way that intimidates others or hurts them. We need to make sure our loved ones feel loved too, and that people feel safe with us.

Emotions are messengers from our body, to tell us what's going on for us. Fear tells us that there may be danger about. Anger tells us someone is infringing on our rights or boundaries. Hurt tells us someone has rejected us.

And so, ideally, take the *message* and bring it to the person (if appropriate), rather than taking the *emotion* to them. So, if you get angry when someone is hours late, the anger is bringing it to your attention. The conversation, ideally shared calmly, is about their lateness and the worry or disrespect you feel when that happens (or whatever is going on for you).

If you do get upset and lose your temper with them, do your best to make sure what you say isn't abusive or nasty. Use 'I' words rather than 'you' words for example. But ideally in a respectful relationship losing your temper should be absolutely the exception, I think. And for sure, apologise to them afterwards for the way you said it. You can absolutely still stand by *what* you said, and your right to have that issue sorted, while apologising for *how* you approached it.

As I become aware of my emotions I often find I am unreasonably upset about things. What I do then is to own and acknowledge the feeling, while realising it's unjustified. The emotions are still valid even though their basic premise is wrong.

So I feel the emotions and acknowledge them, and even share them if appropriate. I might say, 'I felt angry when you went to the football match instead of spending time with me. I know that anger is fully inappropriate as you are perfect entitled to go to the match, and rationally I am delighted you're enjoying spending time with your friends. But I was angry all the same.'

And even if I didn't say it to the person concerned (and I'd only do that if they were able to hear it without feeling guilty or misunderstand me and think I was trying to manipulate them), the fact that I recognise and acknowledge the feelings to myself, is very empowering.

EFT is very good for expressing emotions, and processing them. So, to continue my previous example, if I was angry about someone going to the football match, I'd tap for that emotion so I could process it and let it go. This has the twin benefit that I am acknowledging the genuine emotion (not denying it or repressing it), and letting it go painlessly, and doing all that without inflicting it on the other person too.

Hugs,

Danu

Are you just running away?

Dear DONM ...

A DONM wrote to me the other day asking, 'But if I go No Contact, is that just running away rather than staying to deal with the situation?'

It's a good question of course. It does feel like running away doesn't it? It can feel like a selfish, sulking, pouting, immature '*I'll show her!*' kind of a response.

And it might be, of course. If your motivation is a sulky immature one, then yes, I guess that would be true.

I would venture to guess though that that is a rare reaction. I've certainly never come across it in all these years of communicating with thousands of DONMs. And certainly one who is asking that question, who is worrying about being like that, is not doing it. The immature one would not be second-guessing herself like this.

So, to the sincere ones (which is all of you I have no doubt), I say this:

All the DONMs I have spoken to have considered No Contact when all else has failed. When they have tried and tried and *tried* to solve the situation for years and years and *years*. When they have sustained emotional cuts and bruises and injuries in the process of trying to connect with their mother and solve the problems in the relationship.

So, it's not a case of running away rather than staying to deal with the situation. It's running away (although I'll come back to that phrase in a minute), after having spent years trying, and failing, to deal with the situation. It's running away after years of being the only one trying to heal the situation while your mother went on gaily in her own selfish way. It's running away when you sadly, but realistically, acknowledge that the situation cannot be resolved, and certainly not by you.

And therefore, it is not *running away*. That is a very emotive and even self-judgemental term. It has implications of immaturity and abandoning ship at the first sign of trouble.

I would sooner say that what you are doing is to calmly and realistically accept that this situation cannot be solved, that you deserve to be free of abuse, and therefore you are removing yourself from the clutches of an abuser.

And if someone – probably you to yourself – says, '*Ah that's ridiculous, you're just spinning it so you feel better about it*'. What then?

Spin is inaccurate slanting of a situation to put it in a favourable light. In this case I believe you would be looking at the facts clearly rather than spinning. She *does* abuse you. You *have* spent years trying to sort it out. You *have* consistently failed. You *do* realise now that because she's narcissistic she cannot and will not change. You realise you deserve to be treated well and not abused. Therefore you have no choice but to remove yourself from the situation.

That's the reality of being the daughter of a narcissistic mother. It's not spin.

If anything, the statement that you are running away rather than dealing with the situation is spin. Negative spin, informed by the years of psychological abuse that make you see everything from her angle and nothing from your own.

So, no, I don't think it's running away rather than dealing with it. I think it's calmly and appropriately walking away from an abuser.

Narcissists make it 'My way or the highway', and it's reasonable to choose the highway when they are forcing such a binary choice.

Hugs,

Danu

What if you're wrong about her?

Dear DONM …

People often write to me and say, 'But what if I'm wrong about her being narcissistic? Am I being so unfair to her?'

Here's the thing: you might well be wrong. We all might be. My own mother might not be narcissistic (and wouldn't that be ironic when I literally wrote the book about it!) – it's only my best guess after all, and a fully unqualified guess at that.

However, it seems to me that Narcissistic Personality Disorder is a good model to work with to explain her very real behaviours. Those aren't my imagination. They really happened. The toxic and dysfunctional behaviour continued all my life right up until my very last encounter with her. She never tried to resolve anything in our relationship but worked to overwhelm me and put me back into my box whenever I tried to look for better treatment. The relationship was consistently hurting me and bad for me.

So maybe there's another explanation for those things other than her being narcissistic. But you know what, it doesn't matter. It doesn't change anything in the real world. I still am entitled to protect myself from her consistently abusive behaviour regardless of what label we use for that behaviour.

So yes, I think it's not necessarily that important to know for sure if she's narcissistic. You probably will never know, in truth, as she's unlikely to ever be assessed professionally. All you can do is do your best to make sense of the messy and toxic situation, and as I say, Narcissistic Personality Disorder is a useful handle for it.

So don't fret over it, is my suggestion. If her behaviour was bad enough that you went looking for information, then things are not right in her treatment of you, and that's the important point.

Hugs,

Danu

But what if she *does* apologise?

Dear DONM …

One of the tenets of this narcissism thing is that they never apologise.

And so, what happens if she does actually apologise? Does it mean she's not narcissistic? Does it mean you were wrong all along, and have misjudged her? Does it mean you have to forgive her and go back to where you were with her?

The thing is that narcissists are masters of what we call the *fauxpology* – the fake apology.

One classic method of doing a fauxpology is to say, 'I'm sorry you were upset.'

At first glance this looks like an apology because it has the words, 'I'm sorry' in it, but it really isn't. It owns no fault at all. It doesn't acknowledge she did anything wrong in the slightest. I go into more detail on this in my book *You're Not Crazy*, so I won't repeat myself here.

I wish to speak here of something I didn't say in the book: What if she *does* apologise better than that? A DONM wrote to me the other day with this exact query. Her mother had written to her and said, 'I am sorry for all that I did wrong.'

This seemed to the DONM to be a full apology. It referenced what the mother did, not what the daughter might be feeling, after all.

You might feel under pressure to accept such an apology. If you don't accept such a comprehensive and full apology, aren't you now the wrong one? Aren't you the one bearing a grudge and being unfair?

I don't think so.

The thing is that on the face of it, this seems like an apology. But the apology is so vague as to be useless. It's a blanket get-out-of-jail-free apology that mentions no specifics nor promises any change in behaviour going forward.

So it's not an apology at all. It's more manipulation.

If you want to call her bluff, either to give her every chance, or to satisfy yourself you've done all you can, you can go back to her and say something like: 'Thank you so much for that apology. I would like, however, that you give me specifics of what you are apologising for, so as I know what you think you did wrong and what you still think you were right about. And then we can have a discussion on how we deal with similar situations in future.'

And then wait for the explosion:

'I apologised, what more do you want? You want me to list every little thing I ever did wrong? You enjoy seeing me humiliated? You want to shame me and abuse me and make me feel awful.' And so on.

The details may change but that, I bet, will be the essence of it.

And so, it's not an apology. She isn't acknowledging any specific wrongdoing. She isn't making any promises to change. She is just trying to manipulate you into coming back for more abuse. You don't have to fall for it.

Hugs,

Danu

Drawing lines with narcissists

Dear DONM …

Another favourite trick of narcissists is to lightly, or even kindly, say, 'Let's draw a line under it and move on from here.'

It being some disagreement you're having, no doubt about her behaviour. You may be sure that if it's *your* behaviour that's in question there'll be no lines suggested!

In a way this is first cousin to the 'be a bigger person' gambit we spoke of before. The difference is that it would be the enablers who ask you to be a bigger person, and she herself who is extremely keen to draw lines.

When she talks about drawing lines and moving on, it sounds fair, right? Sounds reasonable. People do this all the time to move on from a small disagreement and carry on with their relationship. It'd be very begrudging to refuse that request. You'd be clinging to your upset and hurt most unjustly. You'd be in the wrong to do that.

And that is the trap your narcissistic mother has set for you. Yes, it is reasonable in most circumstances, when it's two genuine people who care for each other and value the relationship above petty misunderstandings. Or if it's the injured party who says it, as a kind of forgiveness and letting go.

But as is the case in most things, narcissists subvert and pervert this for their own gains. They are not putting the relationship first; rather they are trying to get away with what they've done without consequences, or even acknowledgement. They're trying to get away with it, without making any promises to change their behaviour in future.

They're doing their usual in other words. They're using whatever they can in order to keep abusing you.

And if you say, 'Well it'd be great to move past it, but we need to sort it out first, and find a better way of operating in future', then the temper will come out and the narcissist will show her real feelings.

She wants her get-out-of-jail-free card and she doesn't want you holding her to any standard of behaviour whatsoever. This line-drawing is just a ploy.

Up to you of course whether you play along with it or not. But I think it might help to at least be aware of what's happening and acknowledge to yourself that you are accepting her manipulations for the sake of peace, rather than what you might feel now – confused and bewildered, and feeling bad about yourself for having borne a grudge or whatever the alternative to line-drawing is in her estimation.

In truth though, I think that as long as you are dealing with a narcissist, trying to discuss stuff is a waste of time. If you get to the stage of line-drawing, you've already got caught up in a power battle and it's inevitably one you're going to lose.

Your only options as I can see them are to either suck it up, or to set consequences as we discussed before. Just as you don't have discussions with a toddler or a dog you're training – you put simple consequences in place and wait for them to learn it – it's the same with narcissists.

All fun, eh?

Hugs,

Danu

Dealing with others' judgement isn't easy

Dear DONM …

One thing that's very hard to deal with when you're trying to free yourself from the toxicity of the narcissist, is that she will of course smear you to everyone. She will for sure spin a good story, sprinkling enough truth that it sounds plausible, and people will judge you badly. Your good name will be in tatters.

The people who judge you may well be the people you care about - your extended family, family friends, the congregation at your church, and so on. And they might well also be people you don't really care about – casual neighbours, your mother's hairdresser – anyone she can spin the pity story to really, as of course she's going to get lots of drama mileage about her ungrateful daughter abandoning her or being cruel to her, and so lots of people will hear this.

And it really, really isn't nice to be badly judged. Of course it isn't. We're a social species who depend on relationships for our survival, and so good harmony is an absolute core need. In most cases your mother cannot impact on all your relationships, nor your income etc., but we are still at heart the humans who first evolved to live interdependently in small tribes, so the fear and stress of being rejected burns deeply.

People often write to me and ask how they can avoid this and my answer to them is this: You can't.

Maybe in some few cases, with people close to both you and your mother, you can pre-emptively tell your story.

However, if we try to tell our side of the story pre-emptively, we can come across as nasty and bitter and all sorts. I don't know why narcissistic mothers can tell their tales and inspire pity rather than judgement, why they don't come across as nasty and bitter, but somehow they manage it. Perhaps they play the pity card we wouldn't stoop to, perhaps they spin it as 'my poor daughter, I don't know what's got into her'. I don't really know, but I do know they manage to get more sympathetic ears than we normally can.

So telling people pre-emptively is fraught and perhaps not a good solution.

And we rarely get the chance to tell our side of the story after she has told hers. People don't tend to come to us looking to hear our truth.

And so, the stark truth is that we can't prevent it. Part of the price of our freedom (whether that's total freedom as in No Contact, or emotional freedom as in changing our behaviour around her), is others' censure and judgment. No two ways about it.

So, bluntly: You have to choose which price you'll pay – the price of being judged, or the price of continuing to be abused.

Your narcissistic mother has set it up so that one of those will apply, and most likely you cannot overcome that. So you get to choose. It's not a nice choice to have to make, and I take no joy in describing it so bluntly. But it is the reality.

As ever, there is no right or wrong about what you choose. Whatever works best for you in your specific circumstances is the right thing to do.

But hopefully, seeing the options laid out like this will make the decision somewhat easier. That is my wish for you,

Don't forget that you can use EFT to help you decide, and also to cope with the sting of people's judgement.

Hugs,

Danu

Who are you in her presence?

Dear DONM …

In this chapter I want to talk about identity.

My mother often made it clear that she didn't like me. Of course she did, because it is part of the narrative of the narcissist that everything is the other person's fault. She often used to sigh to me, even when I was a child, 'I love you but I don't always like you.'

Thanks, Ma.

(Actually, I never believed that she loved me either. I somehow always knew, deep down, that she didn't. As we spoke of already, when someone says they love you, it should feel like they do, and it never ever felt like that.)

The thing is that I was a good child, too. As most of us DONMs are. We're always looking for their approval and so we make damn sure to be good. And indeed, it was acknowledged in my home that I was the good one, but even so, any small thing seemed to provoke the 'I don't like you' message.

But the thing is, in the later years of my relationship with her, I found that whenever I was in her company I became someone whom I did not recognise and did not like. The stress of dealing with her and my father was so great that despite my best efforts, some of that stress leaked out, causing me to react snippily and sharply.

I don't see how I could have done differently, however. I was in a total no-win situation. They (my father as well as my mother) were treating me as badly as they pleased, and any attempts of mine to discuss it with them ended up horribly.

So as long as I was in that toxic situation my only options were to endure, and, being human, my endurance was not 100 per cent successful, and so the anger and hurt and exasperation and pain leaked out more than I would have liked.

No matter that I swallowed 95% of the hurt and comebacks and challenges and arguments that she provoked, the other 5%

leaked out despite myself. And so I became snippy and sharp sometimes, which is not like me. And I became closed down and my normal animated self would disappear to be replaced by a stony-faced person.

This was perhaps the most subtle and yet most damaging aspect of the toxic relationship, not so much who she was to me (which was bad enough of course), but who she made me be to myself. I did not like the person I was in her company. The toxicity and stress of the relationship caused me to react in ways that were not who I am. Not often, and not badly, but enough that it distressed me.

And so, one of the many gifts of No Contact is that I do not have to experience that shut-down and snippy and unhappy person any more. I am free to be the person I really am.

And I am sharing this in the hope it might resonate with you, that it might make you realise how you are in your mother's presence that you are not at other times. That you might realise that that person is not you, just the mask you have to wear to be able to survive the toxicity. And that you are able to compare and contrast and realise just how you are different in her presence (if indeed you are), and know who you really are.

Hugs,

Danu

Why we need to believe our parents are essentially good

Dear DONM …

I know from my reading on child psychology that children need to believe their parents are good. This is because parents (or other carers) are essential to a child's survival. And so the child needs to believe the parents are good enough to ensure their survival. If the child were to allow herself to realise some parents are not good, it would be too terrifying as then she would have to accept that her own survival could be in doubt.

Of course, if the parents are bad, the child's survival is at risk anyway, but it's too traumatic for the child to even consider that.

And so a child blames herself, rather than her parents, for their cruelties.

Another reason for this is because if it is the child's fault, then she can do something to fix it. She has (in her mind) the power to change the bad situation. If it's the parents' fault, then the child is truly powerless and it's too traumatic to even begin to accept that either.

And this is partly why we DONMs have such difficulty even seeing the abuse that was done to us. We are in denial.

The other reason is gaslighting of course. We are told early and often that it's all our fault, and of course we believe it, children being disposed to believing their parents. This, too, is a survival mechanism as, with good parents, it makes sense to believe them and trust in their greater wisdom.

So, with our mother/parents lying to us, and our own nature lying to us, it's no wonder that we struggle so hard to see the truth. In my experience, the most common time that women realise it is when they're in their 40s. It takes 4 decades of abuse before we can realise it.

And for sure it's a liberation when we realise the truth. But it's traumatic too, of course. It's a huge step to acknowledge that despite our strong wish and fervent belief, our mother/parents was/were *not* good.

This, too, is why it's so hard to share this information with siblings. They have their own investment in their belief about the parents' goodness, and may not be ready to hear it.

It all makes sense when you see it from this perspective. And so I think it's good to be gentle with ourselves, and with others, when we or they are slow to be able to allow the truth.

Hugs,

Danu

Others' reactions when you try to tell them about Narcissistic Personality Disorder

Dear DONM …

We've spoken about how children need to believe their parents are good.

I suspect that this works on a societal level as well as an individual level.

In other words, I mean that we as a society apply this need to believe in parents' goodness, not only to our own parents, but to parents in general.

A world in which parents are bad and cruel and abusive is not a world we feel safe living in. And it's true that people do know there are bad parents out there; the news leaves us in no doubt about that. But somehow we manage to see those as the odd exceptions, and all other parents as good. Our need to believe is so strong that we are willing to lie to ourselves.

As I said before, I have read that the reason we have fairy stories about wicked stepmothers rather than wicked mothers is so we can speak of the horrible things mothers can do while retaining the myth of the perfect mother, and that makes sense to me.

And so, the result of this is that our friends can struggle to believe us when we speak of our narcissistic mother's cruelties.

The subtle cruelties are so deniable. And it doesn't help that often it is so insidious that it's hard for us to even explain.

If we say, 'She said it was great I'd lost weight, but she had *that* look in her eye that meant she was really furious,' they're likely to say we imagined the look. Because what mother wouldn't be delighted with her daughter looking good?

If we say, 'She said I'd lost weight, but that was her way of reminding me how much weight I've put on,' they'd think we were looking for insult.

And then if we try to share the more overt cruelties, they

just don't believe it. They simply cannot conceive of a mother being so proactively cruel.

So if we say, 'She ironed a hole in my prom dress an hour before I was due to go out in it,' they insist it must have been an accident.

If we say, 'She poisoned my dog because she couldn't bear that I got love and joy and comfort from him,' they'll wonder about our sanity, and explain that dogs get ill and die by themselves.

And so, even well-meaning friends can invalidate us. Not cruelly or abusively as our mother does, but for the above reasons. The result is the same though: we are invalidated, and that is hard when probably the very thing we are looking for most is validation.

I'm torn as to what is the best thing to do in this case. I think the ideal is that we do not seek validation from our friends. It's difficult in most cases for them to give because of this societal belief, and in a way it's not their job either.

But having said that, I do think it's very worthwhile to speak the truth about Narcissistic Personality Disorder. Most people don't know it exists, or if they have heard of it they vaguely think it's got something to do with vanity. The more people who know about Narcissistic Personality Disorder, the harder it is for narcissists to get away with it. As it is, they hide in plain sight as so few people know about them.

So the trick, maybe, is to inform rather than look for validation. To share the information calmly, without expecting any specific response. Easier said than done I know ... I am just exploring all this myself and don't pretend to have absolute answers. But hopefully you will have got some perspective out of my thoughts.

Hugs,

Danu

Narcissists hide in plain sight

Dear DONM …

As I mentioned in the last letter, narcissists get away with so much because so few people know about Narcissistic Personality Disorder. They get away with their lies and manipulations and tantrums and ego trips and abuse.

Now that I know about Narcissistic Personality Disorder, whenever I meet anyone new, especially anyone who might want to be part of my life, I assess carefully if they are narcissistic or not. And there have been a few cases where I have clearly realised someone is narcissistic, and I remove myself quietly from their company.

But others, those who don't know about Narcissistic Personality Disorder, cannot do that, and it leaves them vulnerable and open to the narcissistic abuse. And narcissists are very good at what they do – seducing their victims (either literally in the case of lovers, or metaphorically) to get them hooked and under their control so the fun and games of the abuse can begin.

Or, in the case of mothers and fathers, they don't do the seduction thing as they start ahead of the game – with their victim in their clutches.

As we have discussed, people find it hard to believe that mothers can be cruel, because they're predisposed to believing mothers are good. But also, it doesn't help that if they don't know about Narcissistic Personality Disorder, they don't understand why someone would be cruel and nasty in those petty and immature ways.

It makes perfect sense once you understand Narcissistic Personality Disorder, but until then it seems unbelievable.

The thinking seems to be like this: Why would someone go to the trouble of deliberately ruining your prom dress (to use my previous example)? What's in it for them? Why would they make you miserable at no gain to themselves?

And for sure, it doesn't make sense until you know about Narcissistic Personality Disorder.

So let's tell them about it.

But people, I find, don't want to know about Narcissistic Personality Disorder. They don't want to know that such senselessly nasty people are among us. That is changing somewhat as Narcissistic Personality Disorder has moved a little bit more into the public consciousness, but still, the overall sense is that most people don't know about it.

And so, those of us who talk about Narcissistic Personality Disorder can be like the heroes in 1950s B-movies. There are aliens among us, pretending to be human, passing so well that they fool almost everyone. But those few of us who know the truth try to tell the others and they just don't get it. They think we're mad, or making it up, or taking things out of context, or ... or ... or ...

Whatever it takes for them to keep their illusion that there are no aliens, that everyone is a nice cooperative empathetic human.

I can understand this. Knowing about narcissism is horrible, it's a murky and difficult situation. Far nicer to refuse to see it. But refusing to see it doesn't make it go away. We still have to live with it.

And that is why narcissists get away with so much, because they hide in plain sight and most people refuse to see.

Those of us who know, in that case, can, in small steps, educate the world, if we feel able and up for that (our own safety and healing must come first). In small ways then, this is how we reclaim our power over these narcissists, by slowly cutting off their hiding place.

Hugs,

Danu

Practising saying 'No'

Dear DONM …

We spoke before about being healthily selfish. As a follow-on from that, here's a suggestion for you to take, or not, as you find useful (as indeed, all my suggestions are). I wonder would it be worth your while to practise saying no. Just to get used to it. To the feeling of it, and the process, and the reactions you get.

Not an abrupt or a rude 'no', but a graceful-yet-emphatic one. And you don't have to give reasons either. One of my favourite quotes is from Phoebe in the sitcom *Friends*: 'Oh I wish I could help, but I don't want to.'

Okay, that was for comedic value and I don't suggest you use quite those words but like a lot of comedy it speaks truth through exaggeration, and the basic point is worthwhile: we don't have to make excuses. We don't have to get their agreement or permission to decline the request by coming up with a compelling enough excuse.

One phrase I find helpful is: 'Unfortunately I'm not in a position to do that.' Or, a little more softly, 'I'm sorry but I'm not in a position to do that.'

It's a reason without a reason, in a way. It sounds like you're explaining why you can't, so that you are not offering a blunt abrupt 'No.' However, in reality you're offering no information at all; you're not making any excuses.

One reason why it's good to not explain yourself is simply that you don't owe anyone an explanation. Not wanting to do whatever it is is reason enough. (Obviously if you can't drive an injured friend to hospital, say, I think it's fair to say they'd deserve a genuine explanation. But most of the things you will be asked to do don't fall into that category.)

The other advantage to not giving a reason is that reasons can be overcome. If you say, 'I'm sorry I can't do that as I have to collect Laura from school,' they can insist you'll be finished with their request before it's time to collect Laura.

It might not sit well with you to do this, as you are most

likely trained by your narcissistic mother to never put your own wants or needs first, or even to have put them on the list at all. It might be your default to agree to others' expectations, to almost get their permission before turning down their request. So this concept might be very challenging to you. I obviously don't want you to do anything that's wrong for you, but I do offer you to consider that sometimes it's good to move beyond what is comfortable. What is comfortable isn't always right. Sometimes it's just the bad situation we're used to.

And so, if you agree with this, you could practise playing with the concept of saying no without explanation.

Of course, I'm not recommending you turn into a begrudging selfish woman who never helps anyone, but rather that you seek to flex the 'no' muscle, to practise using it so that you are comfortable with it when you need to. This is about redressing the balance and making sure your 'yesses' come from a place of strength and willingness, not a place of default and obligation.

Another option is to make it a default to say, 'I don't know yet if I'm able to do that; let me get back to you by [some reasonable time in the future].' That way you're not caught on the hop saying yes as a default.

It's still good to practise saying no though! And once you get used to it, the benefits are really good. You feel (or at least, I did), stronger and much more empowered. And also when you agree to do things, you do them with a full heart and don't feel begrudging or manipulated into them. You have more time as you are no longer saying yes to everything, and you are better able to prioritise what is important to you both for yourself and your contribution to your community.

Hugs,

Danu

Why narcissists are never wrong

Dear DONM …

I was thinking recently of *tells.*

A *tell* is a phrase from poker, where bluffing is so important, and players can have a little tic or habit that gives away when they are bluffing. Tapping their forefinger on the table, maybe.

And a huge narcissistic *tell* is that she never admits to making a mistake. Not truly. There might be a faux-admittance in there. *I'm sorry you thought I didn't do it right.* Or, *I'm sorry I didn't do it to your satisfaction.* (The implication being that your standards are unreasonably high rather than her achievement unreasonably low, of course.) Or maybe they'll abuse the passive voice: *Mistakes were made.* But I think even those are rare, and normally you will find that they never ever *ever* **ever** admit to doing anything wrong.

So this *tell*, of never admitting any wrong-doing, is one way you know you're dealing with a narcissist.

It's also one of the many toxicities that makes dealing with a narcissist so difficult. Because, if they never do anything wrong or make a mistake, and something isn't perfect, well then it has to be someone else's fault, right? That's only logic. And the *someone else* may well be you. This applies if the narcissist in question is your mother, or your partner, or a friend, or a colleague.

They'll spin and manipulate things so that it's you who's at fault.

I remember saying once to my own mother, back in the days when I was still trying to work things out with her, that she talks too much, ignoring me and it's not a conversation at all. Her answer? 'Well you make me so nervous that I talk too much as a reaction.'

This is a small but accurate example of how they can spin everything. Others might be:

'You made me do it.'

'You provoked me.'

'Well if you hadn't left the glass on the draining board I wouldn't have broken it.'

What do you do about it? There's not a lot you can do. If it's a work situation then I think it's best to document absolutely everything. If you agree something verbally, send them a quick email confirming your understanding of the conversation so they can't deny it later. If needed you can use their own complaint about you (that you consistently mishear or misunderstand what they said) in order to have the reason for the email: 'As I'm prone to mis-understanding, I'm sending you this to make sure I understood correctly. Please let me know if I got anything wrong and if I don't hear from you I'll take it that this is correct.'

In personal situations, then as far as I can see, you're limited to our usual awful options: suck it up, or remove yourself and go No Contact. By definition they won't change or admit they're less than perfect so …

There are no easy answers to all of this. But at least understanding their patterns arms us better.

Hugs,

Danu

What narcissists will never experience

Dear DONM …

I have written before (in *You're Not Crazy*) of the joy of being wrong, and I'd like to explore that further here.

The one thing I keep thinking is this: I feel so sorry for narcissists. I hate them and despise them and fear them too. The pity doesn't negate that at all.

But I know what they're missing out on, and I do feel sorry for them for that.

I know from my own experience is that there is power and integrity in accepting responsibility when you mess up.

I know there is huge strength in knowing it's okay to mess up, that it's part of being human, and it doesn't mean we are lesser people whenever we make mistakes.

I know that learning and growth and adventure happen on the edges of our lives rather than in the safe centre, and the edge is where confusion and chaos and mistakes live too. I know that there is huge richness in being willing to live at least part of the time on those chaotic edges.

I know that the more comfortable I am with failure, not letting it define me or traumatise me, the more inevitable is my success as, without failure-induced-trauma, it's easier for me to pick myself up and try again.

I know I don't have to live in constant terror of making a mistake and therefore having to acknowledge my own imperfection, because I have already acknowledged that imperfection and live in it daily. Living in the paradox of always striving to improve, but also being okay with who and where I am now. I don't always manage to live this paradox 100 per cent by the way; I mess that up too by blaming myself for doing wrong at times, for example. But that's okay as well. I just strive to do better and improve on that too.

I know all these wonderful things, and I know too that narcissists will never know them. I know that they live in terror of anyone, even themselves, finding out they're less than perfect.

Using my empathy (which they also don't have) I can somewhat imagine that terror and even by my dim understanding of it, it seems like a pure hell.

And in those moments I feel so sorry for these people with their narrow terrified lives. I hate what they do, the chaos and misery they cause, the life sentences they create for their victims. But I can pity them too, and at times I do. And that pity is powerful, because we cannot fear what we pity.

Hugs,

Danu

What if she really does change?

Dear DONM …

One of the truisms we work with is that a narcissist will never change. But people sometimes write to me and ask, 'Yes, but what if she does?'

Because, not often, but it's not unheard of either, a mother will agree to change her behaviour when she has been called on it. What then? It's very confusing for the daughters concerned.

Should they take their mother on face value and work towards a relationship again, they ask? I think that by definition if they're wondering this, their intuition knows it's not right, but at the same time, they want to be fair. And if their problem with their mother was x, or x, y, and z, and their mother has promised to no longer do x, or y, or z, surely they should give her another chance?

I think this one actually has an easy solution.

For a start it's possible that their original guess was wrong, and their mother does not have Narcissistic Personality Disorder. Maybe she genuinely can change, and has changed. So there's an argument for taking her on face value and trying again.

Here's the thing though – a narcissist genuinely cannot change. So if she is a narcissist she will be guaranteed to give herself away, and before too long too.

Either she had no intention of changing, and just said it to draw her daughter back in. Or, she *did* want to change as her desire for her daughter's company was, in that moment when she said it, stronger than her need to do the xyz behaviour.

In the first instance, she won't make any practical attempts to change and will give herself away immediately.

But even in the second case, it won't last. The effort of keeping that change against her nature will be too much for her and she will soon revert to type. Have you ever tried to hold the same poles of magnets together? North-to-North or South-to-South? Picture the effort required to do that, and the fact that as soon as you stop applying the effort, they swivel in the ways they need to go. That's what it's like for a narcissist trying to change. It won't last.

So, I think there is no risk in allowing her to prove herself. You will soon know the truth for sure.

Hugs,

Danu

Narcissists as victims

Dear DONM ...

The interesting thing is that if narcissists are called on their behaviour, they can turn quickly to playing the victim. It's so backwards -- they can do or say what they like to you, but if you call them on it, no matter how mildly or calmly, they react as if you assaulted them.

They might go directly to victimisation, or they might go via the paths of denial (gaslighting), anger/bullying and then onto victimisation.

The gaslighting will take all the forms we've discussed before and you can read about them in more detail on my website: 'I did not say that!' or 'Oh you take everything too seriously'.

If you insist on your point: 'Even so, I would prefer if you didn't mention my weight in front of other people as it really hurts me and upsets me,' she will immediately respond with anger and bullying. This is designed to put you back in your box: 'How *dare* you speak to me like that! I'm your mother!', or, 'Well you think you're so perfect, Missy, let's talk about your faults for a change.'

And if you, heart quaking, continue (as I have done in my time), 'Still, I would prefer if you didn't mention my weight in front of other people,' the victim act will start.

This victimisation, whether they leap to that first, or come to it via the scenic route, will be extreme and frankly, seem like overkill.

All you said was, 'Mum, I really would prefer it if you didn't mention my weight in front of other people as it hurts and upsets me when you do,' and here you are being faced with full blown crying, tears streaming down her cheeks, as she sobs, 'I don't know why you're so mean to me. I can't say anything around you! You take everything I say wrong. I was only trying to help, and this is the thanks I get. I can't do anything right for you!'

For sure the details might not be exact but the script won't vary by much.

And especially, it seems that the worse you're upset, the worse their reaction. Surely, you might think, they would want to comfort you if you're upset, not react so badly? Well no, because … narcissists.

What is going on in their head when all this happens?

I don't know, of course. My best guess though, after years of trying to figure it out when my mother did this, and reading up on it is this: When you show negative reaction to her behaviour – she genuinely *does* feel attacked. It makes sense when you think about it: she believes, and the survival of her whole psyche depends on her continuing to believe, that she's perfect. And here you are pointing out to her that she's not perfect! Of course it's an attack (in her experience).

And the worse your pain, the deeper the implied criticism of her perfection. If you're mildly upset by what she did, she's mildly imperfect, which is bad enough. But if you're deeply wounded, then she's deeply imperfect, and so she cannot possibly allow that reality to exist. She *has* to turn it back to you, to deflect it away from herself.

It does make perfect logical sense, no matter how hard it is to deal with.

And of course it means that the whole topic is deflected because suddenly you're the bad guy. How did that happen? You end up apologising to her, or comforting her. And your own legitimate issue never gets mentioned again, let alone resolved.

It makes perfect sense for them to react this way, as their feelings are genuine but also it serves a very good purpose for them, making sure they're never answerable for their actions.

Hugs,

Danu

Why can't you take criticism?

Dear DONM …

One thing about these clever manipulative narcissists is that they are able to subvert normal things for their benefit. We've spoken about this before, in how they get to create no-win situations. Here is another way they do this. They take something that is a normal part of human interactions, i.e. criticism, and abuse that too.

Their line for this dynamic is: 'You cannot take criticism.'

And that sounds like a valid thing to say. Because it's good to be able to take criticism isn't it? None of us should think we're above that.

(I'm sure you're spotting the irony already. I will come back to this below.)

And so, she gets to criticise you and you have to take it. And you don't understand why it feels so horrible and soul-destroying. Maybe you say to yourself, *Well of course it's going to feel bad, criticism is never fun.*

The trap, of course, is that this is not criticism. It is verbal and emotional abuse masquerading as authentic criticism.

I have been thinking about the difference between authentic criticism and this abuse, and here are my thoughts on this:

Authentic criticism is about what you are doing, i.e. your actions. It is no reflection on who you are as a person. On the contrary, in a healthy relationship it is a measure of their regard for you as a person that they want the relationship to be better, rather than ending it.

Verbal abuse masquerading as honest criticism tells you what the speaker thinks is wrong with *who you are,* rather than what's wrong with what you are doing.

Authentic criticism is designed to get you to change your behaviour in order to function better in your relationship with the criticiser. It's saying, in effect: 'Here is a problem, and you need to solve it.' It will have the solution inherent in the criticism. 'I don't like the way you do x. Could you do y instead?'

Or the solution might be clear from the criticism: if someone complains about you leaving the cap off the toothpaste, then the solution is clearly to put the cap back on in future.

Toxic criticism has no such solution. It doesn't want to solve the problem. It's not aimed at making you improve. Indeed, they don't really want to change the situation as then they'd have no stick to beat you with. Verbal abusers want to keep you squashed and fearful and in the wrong. Toxic criticism is designed to break you and cow you and keep you docile.

And so, because it doesn't want solutions, toxic criticism will be so vague and broad as to be meaningless.

So, the criticism might be: 'You are so over-sensitive.'

Note the words *'You are'* – this is making an absolute statement about you as a person. Note, too, that the complaint is so vague and all-encompassing that it's impossible to know how to fix it. How does this over-sensitivity manifest?

Say you really are over-sensitive. I think a lot of DONMs can genuinely become a little bit over-sensitive. I know I can tend to that myself and it's something I have to constantly watch. It's not surprising when we were living on edge all the time, when we were criticised constantly for who we were, etc. So for argument's sake, let's say that's true and a valid criticism.

In that case authentic criticism would be something like: 'When I occasionally can't meet you, please don't get so upset.'

Do you see how that's specific, and solvable? You can, if you agree there's merit in the criticism, look at your behaviour and come up with some way of handling it better.

But, 'You're so over-sensitive,' leaves you nowhere to go. How do you begin to solve that?

Now, it's possible that even a well-meaning person might not have the skills to articulate what's going on and will resort to the blanket statement such as, 'You're too over-sensitive.' I think though that in this case you could tease it out with them. 'In what ways am I over-sensitive? Can you help me understand?'

I think a genuine person would respond to that, and you both could have a constructive conversation about it, till you get to the root of what's bothering them, and work on a solution that meets both your needs.

I suspect that if you tried that with a narcissistic mother, it wouldn't go so well. She doesn't want to solve the problem, after all; she wants her metaphorical stick to beat you with. So, if you asked her to help you understand, I bet you'd get something like, 'Oh for heaven's sake! I'm not going to be able to give you every example! You're doing it all the time and we'd be here all day if I was to start.'

So that is one way to tell the difference: is it about problem-solving, or about criticism for its own sake?

Or, if the toxic criticism, by some chance, was specific enough for you to address it, you'll find that doesn't work either. They'll either find something else to criticise you about, or will change their mind about what they want. So, for example, if they criticise you for always putting the new toilet paper on the roll the wrong way, and you change how you do it to how they said, then that will become the wrong way and when you say, 'But that's what you wanted,' they'll gaslight you and insist it wasn't.

Even if toxic criticism is specific, it also extrapolates to being about you as a horrible person:

Authentic criticism: *I really would prefer it if you put the cap back on the toothpaste.*

Authentic frustrated criticism: *I hate it when you leave the cap off the toothpaste. I've told you over and over. Please please stop doing that!*

Toxic criticism: *I hate it when you leave the cap off the toothpaste. I've told you over and over. You're so careless. You don't care about my needs at all. You're an absolute loser. You've been a trial to me since the day you were born, I wish I had aborted you.*

Authentic criticism is also about something that's reasonable to ask, whereas toxic criticism will most likely be unreasonable. Okay, defining what's reasonable is a whole other conversation. Is it reasonable to put the toilet seat down or leave it up? That one won't be resolved any time soon!

But although there are blurry parts in the middle, most times the distinction will be clear. It's reasonable to ask someone to text or phone if they're going to be late. It's not reasonable to expect someone to mind-read what you wanted for your birthday and to criticise them if they got the wrong thing when you refused to tell them what you wanted.

So I do offer you the possibility of assessing what criticism you receive to see if it is authentic criticism or toxic criticism. It's good to listen to authentic criticism and assess it to see if it's fair. Toxic criticism is not about you or your behaviour, but about abuse, and so is a very different thing.

And of course, the irony mentioned above is that your narcissistic mother, who thinks it's terrible you can't take criticism, is a person who can never ever take even the gentlest or most reasonable criticism herself. I'm sure you've experienced how any mild criticism of her is greeted with fury and denial and tears and absolute rejection of whatever you're saying. And woe betide the DONM who says to her narcissistic mother, 'You cannot take criticism.' Don't try that at home, folks.

Hugs,

Danu

What about when she's old?

Dear DONM …

What do you do when your narcissistic mother gets old and needs care?

This is a really tough one and I don't pretend to have the answers. I think there are no easy one-size-fits-all answers. But hopefully I can tease through some thoughts which might help.

Bear in mind that as ever, these are just my thoughts and not some expert view or sacred dogma. I will make my case and place my arguments, and if it makes sense to you then that's great, but feel free to disagree with every word. But even if you do disagree with every word and think my arguments don't have any validity, I hope that that disagreement will help you to clarify your own thoughts on the matter.

Also bear in mind that as I discuss this, it is all hypothetical for me. I have not actually been faced with this dilemma.

I have, however, thought long and hard about it because I wanted to be prepared for it if that moment did come. And I share these thoughts here.

I realise that it is very much part of the social contract that adult children look after their elderly parents, and it has been that way since forever, in all cultures. It is a bit blurred these days with pension plans and care homes and so on, but for most of human society we didn't have those, and so the deal was that the parent looked after the child when they were young, and the child returned the favour in due course when the parent became old and helpless in their turn.

My view, however, is that our narcissistic mothers have already broken that deal. She didn't fulfil her half of the bargain. Oh, okay, she did, to an extent. If you're reading this you're still here and so she raised you well enough so that you survived into adulthood. She didn't kill you either through neglect or intention. But that's setting the bar very low, isn't it?

And, I know it sounds like a petulant teenager to say this, but: we didn't ask to be born.

I don't think my son owes me anything for the care and love I poured into his upbringing. To me, it was my decision to have a baby and therefore it was my responsibility and obligation to provide for him, both materially and emotionally. It wasn't a favour I was doing him.

So when I say that it was my mother's decision to have the baby that was me, and therefore it was her responsibility and obligation to care for me, I am being consistent. And, truly, she fulfilled her responsibility very poorly, as did yours.

I don't feel I owe her a damn thing, frankly. I wouldn't anyway, just as my son doesn't owe me anything, but if she had been a better mother and a nicer person and had treated me well enough, I may well have wanted to care for her through love and gratitude. But that situation doesn't apply.

So with the situation as it is, I truly don't think I owe her any care in her old age. I don't wish her ill. I would not be proactively nasty to her. I don't take this decision in a sense of revenge or bitterness. It's just that she is a stranger to me and I am not responsible for strangers' well-being.

Will others judge me for taking that stance? For sure. The belief we should look after our elderly parents is deep in our culture, and I am rejecting that. Of course people will have opinions. And it is part of being human that we want others' good opinions of us. Many emails I get deal with this issue: how neighbours and others will judge the writer if she doesn't look after her mother or parents, and I understand how that social disapproval looms large.

It's up to each of us how we handle that dilemma, because I do not think we can avoid it.

For me, the price of others' negative opinion is a lower price than the price of years of my life and the bruising to my Self that caring for my mother would cost me. It seems unfair that I have to pay any price, but that is the reality, and so I get to choose which price I pay. (As do you.)

And I won't live my life in a way that's toxic to me just to satisfy others' opinion of how things should be done. And those same others, don't forget, don't know the whole story or even part of it. This abuse is a hidden abuse and they do not see it. I would love to explain it to them and therefore get their understanding of my decision and maybe even their approval of it. But that's not possible.

And so I make my choice that I do not owe them care in their older years and I will not be there for them. Quite apart from everything else, I'm still trying to belatedly build my own life, frankly, to repair the damage they have created, to have time or energy for that.

As for what you decide – I do not pretend to know what's right for you. But hopefully this will have helped to clarify your thinking one way or another.

Hugs,

Danu

What about feeling compassion for her?

Dear DONM …

If you do end up looking after her, though, you might struggle with being unable to feel kindness for her. Quite a few DONMs have written to me to ask how to feel compassion for their mother.

Here is what I think about that. (And as ever, judge what I say on its own merits, and see if it makes sense to you.)

My first thought is always about how wonderful these women are, to even seek to feel compassion for their abusers.

And I think how their narcissistic mothers had absolute jewels of daughters and didn't even realise it. That their daughters were diamonds and all they did was heap dirt on top of those diamonds. But the diamonds remain intact, under the dirt, and the narcissistic mother will never know it, in her self-absorption. And how that is her (the narcissistic mother's) loss, no matter that she'll never even know there was something like that to lose. (It's the daughter's loss too, to never be appreciated for the diamond she is, of course.)

So this bruised and abused daughter is still seeking to find compassion for her mother, and I am in awe of that.

About compassion itself, and seeking to feel it and feeling bad if you can't:

My thoughts are that we can feel a kind of distant-compassion, compassion for her physical frailties and the other limitations of age, just as we would for any stranger, but that we are not obliged in any way to feel deep and loving compassion for her.

That kind of thing is the product of a lifetime's healthy relationship and our mothers did not allow that plant to flourish at all. Our lack of compassion is simply the consequences of her behaviour.

So I don't know how you can capture full compassion for her. I am not even sure that you need to try. If you are doing the actions of caring for her, that is a huge and wonderful thing to do for someone who has abused you. I'm not sure you need to beat yourself up over having all the wrong feelings on top of that. The actions are the thing.

It is of course essential to be kind to her and not abuse her in your turn, but I'm not sure that she is entitled to anything more than a distant professional kindness such as a nurse would offer.

And she is lucky to get that, frankly.

Hugs,

Danu

What does Japanese pottery have to do with being a DONM?

Dear DONM …

I recently came across the Japanese concept of Kintsugi. What this means is, when a pottery bowl breaks, they 'glue' it back together with gold lacquer. If you Google the phrase 'kintsugi' you will see beautiful examples.

In this way the cracks are not hidden as if they're something shameful, but rather are celebrated. It's as if they are saying: *This bowl has had a life, and things happened in that life, and we now see the story of those events, and that is fine.*

I think we DONMs can be like this, if we choose. We have been left with dreadful scars by our upbringing. But we can accept and celebrate those scars, and accept them as part of who we are, rather than being ashamed of them. They are part of our lived experience.

For sure, in kintsugi, they fit the bowl smoothly back together. They don't leave it shattered on the ground. It needs to be fit for purpose.

And in the same way we do our best to shape our lives into a smooth and cohesive whole. We pick up the pieces off the floor and shape them into the best life we can. This isn't about living with the breakage.

It's about mending our lives in a proud and assertive way, rather than a furtive and ashamed way. Yes, our lives are pieced together rather than being always whole, but the fixing together is part of us, and to be acknowledged and even valued as such.

Hugs,

Danu

'Stop the silliness'

Dear DONM …

One thing I've seen again and again with these narcissistic mothers that if their daughter pulls away or stops contacting them or whatever, there can be various strategies. One of them is silence as the narcissistic mother waits to see who'll crack first. And it's often the daughter, as she cannot bear the silence, so the intimidation works.

Another one is tears and sobs of: 'I don't know what I've done to deserve this.' Another is playing the victim: 'She's being mean to me.'

But one that comes up again and again is a kind of finger-snapping, 'This nonsense has gone on long enough!' Or, 'Stop this silliness now!'

It might be your narcissistic mother saying this, or one of her Flying Monkeys. But the effect is the same regardless of who the mouthpiece is.

And I have to say I struggle to think of a more arrogant, dismissive reaction. To them, whatever is going on for you to cause you to behave like this, it is not to be taken seriously. Nor is it important to discuss things with you, to ask what's wrong and to try to fix it somehow. Oooooh no. Nope. It is to be dismissed as mere childish sulks.

This totally undermines you, invalidates you and dismisses you. It is also a clear refusal to deal with the issue, and a demand that you return to the way things were before.

It's not surprising of course that she wants things to return like that. The way things were before were working for her. It's how she has it set up, to suit herself. Of course she wants it that way, and is keen that it returns to that way as soon as possible.

And equally naturally, that arrogant authoritarian way of speaking is very intimidating to us. It has been the way we were raised and we are trained to respond to it, and often do. We start believing how she has framed it: that we are being nonsensical, or silly, or absurd, or unreasonable, or however she phrases it.

And so, it's quite likely we'll fall for it and, indeed, stop the silliness.

Except, of course, it's not silliness is it? It's not nonsense. It's what we have been driven to by years of her behaviour and her inability to listen to us or to treat us right.

And her response to *our* reaction to *her* abuse is just more of the abuse – being dismissive and invalidating and resolving nothing.

So it seems to me that it would be good to be aware of how manipulative and inappropriate it is to call someone's reaction silliness or nonsense, and to know we don't have to fall for it.

Hugs,

Danu

Some thoughts on resolving relationship issues

Dear DONM …

Another thought that occurs to me is that in unhealthy relationships nothing is ever resolved. There may be rows – there certainly were between me and my parents whenever I'd try to discuss anything with them, no matter how calmly I'd start.

I'd withdraw, shaking, and then time would pass and next time we'd meet it would be business as usual, no mention of what happened before, and no resolution to it.

And this pattern would repeat over and over. (Why yes, I *am* a slow learner. Why do you ask?)

I think I've realised now that in a healthy relationship, there are three partners in a way. There is you, and me, and the relationship as an entity that we both value. And so if there's a problem, it's a problem within the relationship that needs sorting out, and so both of us will work to do that very thing. It's not about blame as such, or one of us needing to be wrong, but of something not working right. So we approach it in a spirit of problem-solving.

In a toxic or abusive relationship the only thing that matters is 'me' and any complaints are to be quashed immediately so I can carry on as I always have.

In a healthy relationship each person's issues will be taken seriously. They might not automatically be agreed with, but they'll be acknowledged and discussed, not dismissed out of hand.

And so it has become a kind of essential for me in a relationship that if I say, 'I don't like when you do x,' they take it seriously and calmly. My job of course is to say it calmly and not nastily or aggressively. Approaching it as a problem to be solved rather than a personal fault.

And I do go into that discussion knowing I might be being wrong or unreasonable or have too high expectations. I don't for one minute think I'm always right. I try to be for sure. I try to think my issue through myself first to see if I am reasonable to expect this (whatever the 'this' might be), and to resolve it myself, if I'm not reasonable, by changing my own expectations.

But I am aware that even with my best intentions I might be wrong, so I am fully open to discussing it and changing my expectations if that's appropriate.

Likewise if someone comes to me with an issue I do my best to accept it calmly, knowing that to do so is not to automatically assume I am wrong or at fault, but that something isn't working in a relationship I value, so it needs sorting one way or another.

This isn't easy. My immediate default reaction can be a desire to be defensive, and resistant. But as part of trying to be a healthy functioning person in a healthy functioning relationship, I acknowledge that part of me, and reassure myself it's okay, and then try to be present in the discussion.

And so, there is, ideally and usually, no row, but there is a resolution, and we form our relationship rules a bit better, and so it works better going forward.

This is so different from how the narcissists do it. They don't want to resolve anything as we well know. But we are looking for healthier models than that of course and this is one that works for me, and hence sharing it with you to see if you will find it useful too.

Hugs,

Danu

The two-sides fallacy

Dear DONM …

You'll often hear it said: 'There are two sides to every story.'

Or, as a variation: 'There are three sides to a story: yours, theirs, and the truth.'

And people often use this to minimise or invalidate what you are going through with your narcissistic mother.

They might be genuine people who genuinely believe this and are trying to help you as best they can by trying to point out that she's not so bad really, or maybe she didn't mean to hurt your feelings, or whatever.

Or they might be your narcissistic mother's Flying Monkeys who just want to stop you rocking the boat.

But in either case, of course, they are wrong.

There sometimes is absolutely only one side to the story. Sometimes your side is the real truth.

I know that when humans interact there are nuances and misunderstandings and failed assumptions and all sorts that make our communications complex and clumsy and open to failure. So yes, often there are two sides to the story for sure.

Just not when it's a case of absolute abuse such as narcissistic abuse. Or any abuse.

But I think people don't like thinking of abuse. They'd rather think people are well-meaning and it's all a misunderstanding. Or, they don't want their world view rocked by having to know the truth about the abuser. This is why sometimes people even, hideously, do the two-sides thing about sexual abuse: 'What did you do to entice him?' or 'Could you not have said no?'

I think too that DONMs often go too far the way of seeing the other person's point of view. We've been taught that all our lives after all. So when someone says to us, 'Well, there are two sides to a story,' we can find ourselves thinking of our own faults, and how we contributed to the problem.

And truthfully, as humans, we're not perfect, and we're not saying that we are.

But honestly, I think that with narcissists it's pretty much guaranteed that the fault is 100 per cent theirs, or nearly so anyway. Especially since they have us so well trained and so scared so that we make sure to be nice to them and give in to them and so on.

I think we need to keep this in mind when dealing with them, and not fall for the two-sides fallacy. For sure, keep an eye on our own behaviour, as we don't want to fall into the narcissistic never-at-fault fallacy. (Not that I think there'll be much worry about that.) But know that if she's narcissistic she's almost guaranteed to be the one in the wrong, no matter how much she insists she's 100 per cent in the right, and judge accordingly.

And you probably can't stop the two-sides apologists from doing their thing. Flying Monkeys are motivated to keep to the party line, and the genuine people genuinely do believe it.

But make sure you know the truth and don't fall into the trap of thinking it's equally your fault.

Hugs,

Danu

But she wants me back!
Doesn't that mean she loves me?

Dear DONM …

DONMs often write to ask me this: 'If my mother hates me so much, and is so aware of all my flaws as she keeps sharing them with me, why is she so upset now that I'm not seeing her?'

Why, they wonder, is the narcissistic mother sending Flying Monkeys and/or incessantly contacting her (to the point of stalking sometimes). And her pleas and entreaties sound so genuine. It really sounds as if the narcissistic mother is genuinely missing her daughter.

But surely the narcissistic mother should be glad to be free of such a horrible daughter.

But if so, why is she so devastated?

It doesn't seem to make sense, does it?

And so, the poor DONM's thoughts go round and round like a hamster wheel, trying to reconcile this apparent contradiction.

And often, totally understandably, they start to wonder if they misjudged their mother. Maybe she does really love them after all, and that's why she can't let them go.

Along with this dilemma there's a huge dose of guilt for making her narcissistic mother suffer so much. She hears from the Flying Monkeys just how upset her mother is, crying and weeping and sobbing. No wonder she feels guilty.

Maybe, the DONM thinks, she should go back to her mother and try again and see if the relationship could work this time.

But yet, but yet … and round and round the thoughts go.

This seeming dilemma does make sense though, when you realise what's really going on for the narcissistic mother.

Yes, she genuinely does miss her daughter. But think of it this way: Have you ever seen a cat that brought a dead mouse home, and had it taken away? Remember how the cat is so upset and sad and meows piteously at the loss, and goes around the house trying to find it in corners?

The cat is genuinely missing the mouse. But as its prey, its chew-toy. It does not want a healthy, loving, mutually respectful relationship with the mouse.

And that, I would argue, is an exact analogy of how the narcissistic mother feels.

The narcissist's addiction, don't forget, is to the drug of attention. Narcissistic Supply, as it's called. And if her daughter removes herself, then her mother has lost that source of Narcissistic Supply. No wonder she's devastated.

Add to this the fact that narcissists absolutely *hate* rejection. Okay, none of us likes rejection but narcissists really *really* hate it. They cannot bear it. You could almost say they are allergic to it.

Again, this makes total sense because if they're so perfect, why would anyone want to reject them? And so their daughter walking away is an implicit statement that they're not perfect, and of course narcissists cannot bear that thought.

So, they cannot bear rejection, and now their own daughter has rejected them. The sooner that situation is cancelled out, the better.

Another factor might be that the narcissistic mother is loving the drama. She can weep to all the potential Flying Monkeys about how devastated she is, how bereft, how sad. She can gather lots of attention and sympathy and 'stroking' that way.

So those three factors: the chew-toy factor, the hate-rejection factor, and the love-drama factor, are all real and credible reasons why the narcissistic mother will seek to get her daughter back.

And none of those reasons involve loving her daughter, or respecting her daughter, or missing her daughter for herself. None of those reasons involve any genuine wish or intention to improve the relationship.

If she's narcissistic, she does not love or respect or miss anyone.

My point is that the narcissistic mother's distress is totally genuine, but is not a sign that she loves her daughter. And so, from the daughter's point of view, nothing has changed.

It can be very hard to really really accept that she will never change, and let that hope go. But freedom – painful freedom, but freedom nonetheless – lies in accepting that.

I don't think there are any DONMs who have walked away from their mother on a whim, or at the first sign of trouble. We all walked away after years and years and *years* of trying to sort it out. Not only did the narcissistic mother not meet us half-way, she used our well-meaning efforts as a way to further abuse us. That's the reality. And all her tears and phone calls will not change that.

Hugs,

Danu

What about drama queens?

Dear DONM …

Today I'm going to talk about drama queens.

You know what I mean, I am sure, about drama queens.

They are the ones who love drama, and crisis, and upset, and who will provoke such things in their own lives because of the attention they can get for it.

They even love trauma and tragedy, once those are happening to other people but they get to witness it. They love to help but this help is voyeuristic and self-important, giving them a ring-side seat. (This is, if the help does actually offer the best views. If you ask for something unglamorous: 'I'd love some help, thank you so much for offering. I wonder could you cook a few dinners for the freezer?' – you won't see her for dust.)

Drama queens are allergic to peace and quiet and tranquillity, and so, if there isn't enough drama going on, they'll even create some. They'll decide they might have a terminal illness, or get a mystery allergy, or provoke a row with a friend, or decide their husband's having an affair. Anything to create drama.

Or, something that to the rest of us would be just a blip in the day – temporarily losing our keys, for example – will become a crisis of the highest order for them.

Drama queens can even sabotage themselves into losing a job, say, because something like that can provide great drama.

People can be drama queens without being narcissists – it's a trait associated with Narcissistic Personality Disorder's 'sister' disorder: Histrionic Personality Disorder, for example. And perhaps not all narcissists are drama queens. There's definitely a big overlap though. Drama leads to attention, and as we know, narcissists need attention.

Drama queens are exhausting to be around. Most of us prefer to avoid drama as it's stressful and overwhelming, and life brings enough crises all by itself without creating more. So being in the blast zone of all this drama is very challenging.

But yet, but yet, we might feel obliged to help the drama

queen. That's what friends and family are for, right? If someone close to us loses her job or has a bad fight with her husband, shouldn't we be there for her? Help her, listen to her, support her?

It's a bit of a quandary to be sure. And especially since DONMs have been trained to be docile and pleasing.

As a nice person, for sure be there for people when they need you. But if they need you too often, if they just seem so accident-prone and a disaster-magnet, then that might be a flag that they're a drama queen.

Or, while we all want to vent, I think, whenever something major goes wrong, in most cases after a suitable vent, or time to process what's happened, healthy people go about fixing the problem. They might still need your ear, but now they'll be saying things like, 'Do you think Solution A or Solution B would be better?'

The drama queen on the other hand will simply be wallowing in the issue with no desire to fix it.

Likewise, if you come up with suggestions, the healthy person will consider them genuinely. The drama queen will shoot down all practical suggestions immediately. She doesn't want solutions; she wants sympathy.

And just be aware of the tone of it all. A healthy person is genuinely overwhelmed and upset about whatever crisis has happened. A drama queen is enjoying it; there'll be an air of excitement about her.

So how do you handle it?

I tend if possible to ease away from drama queens altogether, so I don't have to put up with them. I am aware that drama queens are manipulative and that they're using people as drama fodder or audiences, so I feel no obligation to be with them.

And if for any reason I'm stuck in their drama without escape I make sure not to feed the drama in any way. I don't agree breathlessly with them that yes, it's terrible, and x is a horrible person and y shouldn't have happened and z is so unfair. I stay deliberately calm and deadpan really. 'I can see you're very upset about that all right. But I have faith that you will be able to overcome it.' (I don't have that faith at all, of course, but it calls their bluff.)

Yes, I risk being accused of being very unsympathetic, but that's okay too. My real friends know I am sympathetic and supportive, and if a drama queen doesn't think so, well she won't try to milk me for sympathy again, which is a win in my book.

Hugs,

Danu

We are the Bonsai Children

Dear DONM …

Those of us who were raised by narcissists are the Bonsai Children.

    The seed that was us was just as whole and full of glorious potential as every other seed. We had the wondrous vibrant audacious potential to grow deep roots to embrace the earth and spread exuberant branches to hug the sky. But we were not planted into freedom, into rich earth, with room for our roots to firmly claim our share of the earth, and to anchor ourselves solidly, and from there to grow upwards, strong and sturdy, reaching for the sky, branching out, green and vivid and hearty.

    No.

    We were planted into a tiny pot. It might even have been a pretty pot, a ceramic pot with cute round feet and curlicues and swathes. It might have been an ugly pot, cracked and broken terracotta. But it was for sure a constraining, limiting, shackling pot. Our roots were limited, growing only a miniscule distance before they reached the cold hard uncaring limits of the pot. And so they had no choice, these roots, but to remain tiny puny things with only a tenuous hold on the tiny parcel of earth they had been allocated.

    And some of us were watered well in that pot, and fed well. We were still stunted though by the inherent limits of the pot. Others of us were not even given enough of our basic needs with inconsistent watering and very little food, so the stunting came from many angles.

    With our roots so limited, and possibly our needs barely met, how could we grow tall and strong and solid?

    We could not.

    But just to be sure we did not grow to our potential, our twigling shoots were ruthlessly clipped and pruned to keep us small. Our tiny hopeful branches were wrapped in tight coils of harsh cold metal which were then twisted and manipulated to make them grow in the shape desired by our creator.

This desired shape being an imitation and a mockery of how we would look as adults, if left to grow freely. The desired shape of another, to whom our very existence, our very shape, our reality, was a matter for their whim and preference over our own true needs.

From the thin artificial soil of our pots we could see other trees. We saw how boldly and unapologetically they grew tall and strong. But even as we looked in awe and envy at the real trees, we did not realise that that was our birthright too, stolen from us.

We did not even realise we could aspire to grow as robustly. We thought that such strength and beauty was for other trees, better trees.

And so, we were small and weak and stunted and hobbled, and we blamed ourselves for it.

A double pain. To be so less-than, and to be at fault for that. So many layers of shame.

And indeed our creator blamed us too, if we dared to question it. *You'd never grow big and strong*, they'd sneer. *You're lucky we kept you at all. You're lucky we watered you when other trees access their own water. You're lucky we fed you when other trees work for their own nutrients. You are pathetic and you dare to question us who have given you everything?* And it seems true; it seems plausible, so our meagre branches bow lower, and our tiny leaves quiver in the heat of the breath and spittle of their anger.

This is what it means to be a Bonsai Child.

The biggest leap we'll ever take is the mental leap of knowing that the pot is not our true home, the metal binds not our true clothing. After that there's the physical leap to leave the pot and claim our birthright. But we carry the years of stunting with us, struggling to recover, to grow as strong and tall as the other trees do effortlessly. And maybe blaming ourselves for that struggle, not realising that it's the grotesque legacy of being one of the Bonsai Children and none of our doing at all.

And we forget to applaud ourselves for having left the pot and for trying to grow beyond the pruning at all.

Until we remember.

Hugs,

Danu

The quest for her approval

Dear DONM …

One thing that every DONM needs to realise for her own peace of mind is that she will never please her mother. (Or at least, not to a large extent and not for long – I speak more of this below). This is a hard, and sad, fact to accept, but peace and even a kind of freedom comes from accepting it. You can let down the burden of trying to win her approval, and only then will you realise just how exhausting that burden was.

So why can't you please her, no matter how hard you try?

The fact is that she doesn't want to have you please her. That is too easy and too harmonious and too drama-free.

She wants you on edge and anxious. She wants you vying for her approval. When you are hungry for that approval, you are focussing on her and giving her attention, and she's happy with that situation.

The promise of her approval is the bait she wields to keep you trying. But like the carrot on the stick in that famous image of the donkey, the bait is always out of reach.

Okay, she might well drop you a few crumbs of approval now and again, the amount being carefully judged to make you hopeful that her overall approval is an achievable goal. Much as casinos allow gamblers a carefully calculated number of wins, because if we always lost, we'd eventually give up. And of course your mother doesn't want you giving up on your quest for her approval, so she will give small and temporary approval when needed.

My own mother used to say, her tone full of approval, 'Oh you're *soooo* good to do that!' – whatever 'that' was. Things like bringing her in food every day to hospital because she didn't like the hospital food, is one example I recall.

And as I think of it, the actions that gained her approval most were those that stroked her need for Narcissistic Supply. Bringing her food that I had cooked meant I was thinking of her while I cooked, and all the other patients in the ward got to see that she was getting special treatment.

The time my sister and I spent hours cleaning her kitchen from top to bottom when she was out (she wouldn't have been a great housekeeper to say the least), didn't garner nearly the same amount of approval. No, instead she was furious. Absolutely furious. She didn't say so of course. She couldn't. She said thank you, briefly and begrudgingly, because she had to. But I could tell she was furious by her scowl and the fury emanating from her in almost-visible waves. It took me years to figure that one out but of course it was because us cleaning the kitchen was by definition an implied (even though unintended) criticism of her housekeeping skills.

But she would approve whenever I did anything to stroke her narcissism.

Whenever she said 'You're *so* good to do that,' it used to stress me unbearably. This was long before I knew about Narcissistic Personality Disorder, or even before I'd acknowledged things weren't good, so I could never understand why I found it painfully difficult.

I think now it's that I realised that that approval was so incredibly conditional. It was approval of that one action I had done, rather than any approval of who I am as a person. That approval was so temporary, and fragile. That approval would be withdrawn fully and instantly the next time I didn't please her.

And, the disapproval was about who I am rather than whatever 'bad' thing I had done. Being bad and disapproved of was my default state it felt, and I was always trying to move away from that.

I now realise that was doomed to failure. Like that Greek chap in the legend, Sisyphus, who was doomed forever to roll a stone up a hill, only to have it roll back down again to the bottom just before he reached his goal.

This need for her approval is a powerful weapon she has over us, and it's one she brainwashed us with from our earliest days.

However, this belief only has the power we give it. We can't help the fact she brainwashed us with it, but we can reject the brainwashing now and choose to get our approval from ourselves instead of her.

I am talking about approval of who we are as people, and that's our birthright I think. It doesn't mean we're perfect (because we're not). It means we're okay despite not being perfect. As one DONM wrote to me the other day: *We're imperfectly and wondrously made.*

Sisyphus was stuck with his task, but the good news for us is that we can stop doing ours. We can just stop trying. Easier said than done of course, but as ever you can use EFT to help you. And as I said at the beginning of this letter, the freedom and release and peace you will feel is incredible.

Hugs,

Danu

What do toddlers and narcissists have in common?

Dear DONM ...

I have realised one thing about narcissists: Whatever the question is, the answer is 'toddler'.

I mean this as a metaphor of course. But also I think it's more than that – that narcissists are factually and genuinely still mentally and emotionally toddlers.

Toddlers think the world revolves around them. They struggle to see the difference between wants and needs. They have no sense of deferred gratification; when they want something, they want it now. They have no empathy; they cannot see how others might feel about things and therefore don't care about mistreating others. They will be sunny and cheerful when they get their way but turn to instant sobs and tantrums the minute they're thwarted. They have a rich fantasy life, being certain that if they think it's so, it must be so. And more, if they say it's so, it must be so.

Does any of this sound familiar? Can we replace the word 'toddler' with 'narcissist' and have it still make sense? I think so.

Like toddlers, narcissists, particularly those on the milder end of the scale, can be genuinely fun and cheerful and pleasant to be around, right until they're not of course. But once their narcissistic need for attention is met, and their ego is being stroked, they can be rather lovely.

This is partly why we can have the confusing experience of thinking, as people often write to me: 'But she can be so nice!'

Of course she can. But the thing to remember is that it's only paper thin niceness. It's a niceness caused by having everything her own way.

But both toddlers and narcissists have meltdowns when things don't go their way. We call it a tantrum when it's a toddler, and narcissistic rage when it's a narcissist. But they're pretty much the same thing.

The horrific thing is that these toddlers-in-adult-bodies have power over their own children. Can you imagine a toddler being in charge of a household? What a terrifying scenario.

Of course, you don't have to imagine it. You lived it.

Hugs,

Danu

When people gush about how nice she is, what do you do?

Dear DONM …

What do you say to people who aren't Flying Monkeys as such, but who wish to talk about your mother? Maybe people who are genuine, but who have her bending their ear about the fact you aren't in touch, and who are therefore caught in the middle.

I think that you would be justified in saying to them that this is nothing to do with your relationship with them and so you ask them not to speak to you about your mother to you.

Furthermore, I would also say that that they are in their turn entitled to say to your mother that they're not getting in the middle and do not wish to hear any more about you from her, as sometimes people genuinely don't realise they're allowed to not be part of a conversation they don't want to be part of.

But regardless of what they do, you don't want to hear any more about her and your relationship with them has to be independent of that. (Of course, say it more softly and diplomatically than that, but that'd be the bones of it.)

And of course when I say that you 'ask them' to not speak to you about her – I am suggesting that that is the way you phrase it. In fact of course you are telling them this and will enforce it via boundaries if needed. If they insist on talking to you about her then they do fall into the category of Flying Monkeys and need to be dealt with accordingly.

If you meet casual acquaintances who know your mother and gush about her, then it's slightly different I think. Often narcissists can come across very well in a superficial way – they make it their business to do so, so they can get the approval and admiration they want. And in superficial relationships they can hide their real selves, so people don't see through them.

So you might well have people gushing as I say: 'Oh I loved your mother! She was such fun! So nice!'

I've had this, and the temptation to tell the truth is very strong.

But I just gritted my teeth and said lightly that I was glad they had such good memories of her; that she'd love to hear that. (That last bit was true, as she would love to hear it. But it wasn't a promise to tell her either!)

The real situation with my mother is not for sharing with casual acquaintances, and so I will just thank them for their kind words and let it go, frustrating though that is.

Sometimes, though, you do want to try to explain, and we talk about this next.

Hugs,

Danu

So how DO you explain narcissistic mothers?

Dear DONM …

Sometimes close friends really want to understand, and we can struggle to know what to say.

Here is my attempt to explain it. If you find this useful by all means copy it to give it out to other people.

Narcissistic mothers do the opposite of what real mothers do:

Where real mothers build us up, narcissistic mothers knock us down. They either do it deliberately, for the pleasure of that, if they're malignant narcissists, or just carelessly, as collateral damage to their own wishes.

Real mothers provide a soft place for us to fall, when their daughters are down and weary. Ours begrudgingly provide a barren concrete slab. Or maybe a mattress of barbed wire, for the fun of adding to our misery. And they'll never stop reminding us of how they helped us.

Real mothers see themselves and their daughters as being on the same side. Our mothers see us as the opposition or the competition.

Real mothers enjoy our company. Narcissistic mothers enjoy our attention.

Real mothers see their daughters' beauty and applaud it. Ours will make sure we know all our flaws.

Real mothers want their daughters to fulfil all their potential. Ours do not want us outshining them. Unless they want us to do well as a reflection on them.

Real mothers rejoice in their daughters' successes. Narcissistic mothers resent them. They might milk them, of course, for attention from others. But they'll resent us for doing so well and any words of congratulations will stick in their throats.

Real mothers have annoying foibles. Ours have toxic and abusive behaviours.

Real mothers mourn for our sorrows. Narcissistic mothers relish the drama of them.

Real mothers delight in their daughters. Ours delight in what we can do for them.

Real mothers are interested in their daughters' lives. Ours have no interest in anything outside themselves.

Real mothers are kind. Ours are completely selfish.

Real mothers are warm. Narcissistic mothers are cold. Except for the heat of anger.

Real mothers hold us in their hearts. Narcissistic mothers hold us in contempt.

Real mothers can be testy and cranky and short-tempered at times. Our mothers are downright nasty.

Real mothers are willing to discuss and compromise. Narcissistic mothers invented *my-way-or-highway-ism*.

Real mothers look for the win-win. Narcissistic mothers insist on the 'I win'.

Real mothers love their daughters. Our mothers love only themselves.

Hugs,

Danu

How do we know what the truth is?

Dear DONM …

I spend my life second-guessing myself, always ready to hear the other side of the story and correct myself if I'm wrong. I remember being in awe of my mother and brother at times, because they were always so certain of their rightness. How could they be so certain, I wondered in some kind of admiration, even as I was frustrated by it and how stubborn it made them. I felt my own fluidity was some kind of personality flaw in comparison. Now that I know better I think my own uncertainty is better, because absolute certainty is arrogance. But, my word, it can get exhausting.

And so for a long time I've struggled with this. What is truth? How do I know I'm right? Maybe I'm not. After all, the other person is being very certain and I'm second-guessing myself. How hard should I insist on my perspective if someone else remembers it exactly opposite?

And I've no absolute answers yet, but here are my thoughts on that:

It is a fact that human memory is notoriously unreliable. This applies to everyone, always, but it applies even more so when the event to be remembered was a very intense and emotional one (such as when the event is some traumatic incident with our narcissistic mother).

What can happen is that we *think* we remember, and indeed are *certain* we remember, because the memory seems so clear. The memory however can be wrong, especially about details.

So if we witnessed a car crash, for example, we might distinctly recall that the car was white, but in fact it was brown. Or we might recall that it went through a red light when it didn't.

It's not that we're making things up. Well, we are, in a way. It's our subconscious mind making it up though, rather than us consciously writing fiction. That's why it feels so real.

So, that applies to everyone.

Add to this the fact that abused children have damaged hippocampuses, which is the part of the brain involved in creating long-term memories, and we DONMs probably have less reliable memories than most people.

So, I feel 100 per cent confident in my memories because they seem so real and so right, but I also know that that 100 per cent confidence is misplaced.

So what is the truth then? How do I know? Especially, how do I know with regard to events involving my narcissistic mother, when she is adamant that they didn't happen the way I said. I'm No Contact with her, but our last conversation included her patronisingly telling me I had a very vivid imagination as a way of denying certain events even happened.

And I have had many many times where she would say, in surprise and wide-eyed astonishment, 'But Danu, that never happened!', sounding so convincing that I'd begin to doubt myself. (Classic gaslighting of course.)

So what is the truth about *anything*? How do I know? And of course, by extension, since these letters are really about you and I only use myself as an example, how do *you* know?

The fact is that you don't. Not 100 per cent. You could be wrong.

But then, so could your narcissistic mother. She is equally prone to remembering incorrectly. Of course she'll never admit this, seeing as she's a narcissist 'n' all, but it's true. A kind of absolute certainty is arrogance, I think.

So, what I do is to try to get evidence if I can, to back me up. I record things, with my camera or a quick note, if it's important. I compare notes with others who were there to check I got it right.

And I accept that I might be wrong. But the thing is that *I might be wrong some of the time, but I surely am not wrong all of the time.* And my narcissistic mother was surely not right all the time either.

The truth lies somewhere in between. And since I genuinely was looking for the truth and was only tripped up by the flaws in human memory, and she was determined to deny the truth if it didn't suit her, I think it's fair to suppose that the truth lay nearer my side than hers.

I also accept that while I may not have been right about all my memories, the law of large numbers applies, in that there were many many events I recall, and even if we take away an arbitrary 10 per cent or 20 per cent of them, the pattern still applies and the overall situation was emotionally and psychologically abusive.

And I know that she has lied (or misremembered if I am to be charitable) about things that I know for a fact were as I remembered them, because I did have corroboration for my memory, from someone else who was there, or some record of the event. So her saying it was x when I recall it as y, carries no weight for me at all even for the things I have no corroboration over.

If someone genuine in my life, such as my son David, remembers something differently to me, then I don't automatically dismiss my own memories, but I certainly don't argue for them either.

More likely he and I will agree to differ on the memory, but discuss calmly and fully whatever the issue was.

So say I remember him snapping at me, but he says he didn't, we can still discuss how we like to be spoken to respectfully and agree on that. We are discussing it only hypothetically if his memory is right and it didn't happen, but it's still a valuable discussion.

So he and I don't need to know for sure whose memory is correct. This works because we have a good and healthy and mutually respectful relationship, and both of us values the other, and our relationship with the other, more than we need to protect our ego.

But that, of course, doesn't apply with narcissistic relationships. And so, for those relationships, to the extent I have to stay in them, I will choose to believe the overall pattern of my memories, even if I know that not every individual memory is correct.

For the rest, I have to come to some kind of peace about the confusion. I have to trust my memories because if you can't rely on anything then that's incredibly stressful, but not to trust them too much. It's a difficult balance and one I haven't quite figured out yet. Perhaps the trick is to be aware of the dilemma and live with it.

There is peace for me in acknowledging the dilemma, though.

Hugs,

Danu

How we can get stuck in the Drama Triangle too

Dear DONM …

I've written on the website about the Drama Triangle with regards to your narcissistic mother. However, it's true that we DONMs can be on the Drama Triangle too, and I explore that here. I invite you to read up on the Drama Triangle on the website to understand the terminology. You'll find it here: http://www.daughtersofnarcissisticmothers.com/narcissists-drama-triangle/.

From the narcissistic mother's point of view we are very often Persecutors but I suspect that it is a rare DONM who is a true perpetrator of violence or abuse towards her mother.

We can end up very stuck in Victim mode though, and also Rescuer Mode.

Regarding being in Victim mode – it's true that we are victims of this abuser. And because of the brainwashing and a psychological experience called learned helplessness, we can stay stuck in that mode. So much of the DONM struggle is seeking to free ourselves from the toxic dynamics that keep us as a Victim.

Also, we can be stuck in Rescuer mode, as I spoke of before when I wrote about how we feel it's our job to keep her happy, and to fix all her problems.

This can happen in two ways. The first is that our narcissistic mother casts us in that role. She makes us responsible for her happiness and well-being. She might even do things such as forget to take essential medication in order to force us into the role of Rescuer. This gives her the benefit of playing the Victim, and also of getting that attention (i.e. Narcissistic Supply) from us. And when we are a Rescuer to her we can feel her temporary approval as I spoke of earlier, with all the baggage and seduction of that.

The other way we can be a Rescuer is to get into Rescue-mode for others too. Being a Rescuer is a much higher-energy state than that of a Victim, and we surely aren't going to be a Persecutors, and we haven't enough healing in the first instance to leave the Drama Triangle altogether, so being a Rescuer is the only other option.

I can clearly see that when I first realised about my mother being narcissistic I went into full-blown Rescuer mode. I am very embarrassed about that now, in truth, but it was a natural evolution to my healing, as it would be for all of us. There was no malice involved in my Rescuing, but from this perspective I can see that it was still very dysfunctional in ways.

It takes a lot for me to share this, as I am, rightly or wrongly, embarrassed and ashamed of it. But I try to forgive and understand myself for it, and to know that it was, as I said, part of the evolution of the healing.

And I share it in the hope that you can realise this about yourself if you are in the same place.

I like to think, and genuinely think, that I have left the Drama Triangle now. Yes, I am still helping by having the website and the other resources such as this book, but my mind-set is completely different. I am no longer so attached to the outcome, I am no longer feeling responsible for everyone's healing, I am no longer getting the same validation from doing it, I'm no longer co-dependent about it all and that, I think, is the difference.

To leave the Drama Triangle, either via a time spent as a Rescuer, or just directly, we need to claim our power, and set boundaries and so on: all the things I have spoken of in these letters.

But yet, and there is no blame attached to this either: the Victim role can be comfortable. It is seductive.

Being a Victim is paradoxically safe. No matter how awful it is, we know our role, our place. We know the script. We know the steps to that dance without having to think about it.

While we are a Victim there is good reason why we can't achieve, why our life is a mess and so on.

And all that is genuinely true. It's not just our perspective. I wrote before about how children of narcissists are Bonsai children, and we are genuinely stunted.

The difference, though, is what we do once we realise that we are in the Drama Triangle. We can stay in the Victim mode, or start to grow out of it. But growing is scary. It's the unknown. While we are the Victim, everything is the Persecutor's fault, but if we grow out of that we have to start taking responsibility for ourselves.

It is terrifying. I know that. I experience that terror every day frankly. I am realising there is a price for everything, and the price for freedom, and autonomy, and maturity, and growth is that we stop being a Victim and claim all responsibility for ourselves.

I truly believe that it is worth it, but I fully acknowledge how difficult it can be and how scary it is. And I often find myself being drawn back towards the Drama Triangle, wanting to feel like a poor little Victim, or wanting to be a Rescuer. I have to be fully aware always of this dynamic, and diligent about avoiding it.

Again, it is worth it though. When I am safely off the Drama Triangle I am fully adult, able to make decisions for my own life and steer it in the way I want it to go. I can be a good helpful friend without letting ego or attachment turn me into a Rescuer. I can do my work in a healthy and loving way without getting an ego trip out of it. Satisfaction, yes, of course, as there must be in any endeavour or why would we do it? But not ego in a dysfunctional sense.

And all those things are good, and I cherish them, and so I am diligent to monitor myself to make sure I stay off it.

And I share this as ever in the hope that you too might find some direction in this, that you might be able to identify if you are on the Drama Triangle, and if so how you might step out of it.

Next I share some ideas for stepping out of the Drama Triangle.

Hugs,

Danu

Some ideas on how to step off the Drama Triangle

Dear DONM …

One thing I've strongly realised about our dysfunctional relationship with our parents, or indeed dysfunctional relationships in general, is how we get stuck in often-repeated scripts and well-worn grooves of responses. And how a stimulus such as an attack from our mother as Persecutor can automatically trigger us into Victim. Or how a stimulus from her as Victim can automatically send us into Rescuer mode.

These are all very well-formed habits, and we keep doing them automatically.

The trick to stepping off the Drama Triangle is to respond differently. To refuse to take the roles of Victim, or Persecutor, or Rescuer.

I think the best way to stop being a Victim is to really own your own situation. To effectively announce to yourself : *'This is where I am. It absolutely is not my fault that I am here. But from now on I will steer my own life without apology. I am not obliged to play the part of anyone's Rescuer. They are responsible for their own life, just as I am. And I do not have to wear the title of Persecutor just because someone else tries to allocate it to me. I choose to know that honestly and ethically living my own life is not abuse of anyone else, no matter how much they try to spin it that way.'*

If she tries to cast you in the role of Persecutor, saying something like, 'You always do x,' or 'You made me feel y,' then instead of defending yourself or apologising, you can say something like, 'I'm sorry you feel like that.' Hey, she's not the only one who can do fauxpologies! And besides, you can be genuinely sorry she's feeling distressed without accepting responsibility for it.

Or if your narcissistic mother tries to cast you in the role of Rescuer, you can sidestep that. If she says, 'You *never* do x for me.' your automatic reaction might be to point out all the times you did x, or to apologise for the sake of peace and promise to do x more/better in future. Both of those responses accept without argument her implicit belief that you need to do x for her. Instead, maybe brainstorm based on your own mother's particular issues and come up with responses which put the ball back in her court for her being an adult for herself. Something like, 'I'm sorry you feel like that. Maybe you could do x for yourself.'

Or, what if, for example, she creates emergencies to force you to come and Rescue her, such as phoning you at some ridiculous hour to tell you she forgot to renew her prescription and needs her medication right now. Up to now the pattern would have been that you would drop everything to help her, phoning her doctor, or pharmacists, to plead with them for help. If you want to stop her manipulating you into being a Rescuer, this has to stop, and you need to let her experience the consequences of her actions as all adults do. If it is something important like medication I think I would help her one last time, but tell her sternly that it is the last time and she is responsible for this in future.

And then, the next time it happens, remind her kindly but firmly that it was her responsibility, and let her experience the consequences. Yes, this is very difficult. She could be in genuine medical distress because of this. But, assuming she's not suffering from dementia, it is her fault and her problem. It is not your problem. You gave her due warning. It is pure manipulation of her to make you take greater care of her health than she does herself, and if you are to avoid the Drama Triangle then you need to refuse to take the responsibility.

(In practice, in a case like this, I think I would set up an automatic reminder email at the time, so that I was helping but not Rescuing. There are services that can do this – just Google 'schedule emails' to see your options. And then set it up so that she gets a reminder email before the old prescription expires.)

If you do fall into emergency Rescue again (rather than the strategic helping which the automatic email would be), you are playing the role of the Victim again. This is a fact, not a value judgement. I do not judge you or think you're wrong to do that, and I hope you don't judge yourself either. It's a fact that you are being a Victim in that you have to do something that you don't want to do and which is not your problem to solve.

And I do not for one moment underestimate how difficult it is to step off the Drama Triangle. Both her strong desires and your strong training conspire to keep you on it.

If you do step off the Drama Triangle, will she be happy with you refusing the roles of Persecutor and Rescuer? Of course not. Far from it. Indeed your refusal to do these things will be seen as more evidence of your badness as a Persecutor. But don't forget that this is only in her perception, and you don't have to let it be yours. This is her song but you do not have to sing it.

More about this next .

Hugs,

Danu

A trick Derren Brown taught me

Dear DONM …

Something that inevitably happens with the narcissistic dynamic is that we get into a situation where we keep replaying the same patterns. And we contribute to that too, as we have been trained to respond in a certain way. We have learned our script so to speak. She says or does x and we say or do y in response.

So when we pluck up our courage to call her on something and she gets upset about it, we rush to comfort her. Which is exactly what she wanted as her upset is pure manipulation to achieve that very aim.

Or when she gets inappropriately angry, we rush to placate her. Which again, is exactly the point.

Or when she ignores us we rush around trying to get her to acknowledge us or speak to us again. Which again, is the idea.

She has trained or programmed us to respond in certain ways, and we produce those responses without even thinking.

Another way of looking at this is to think of your relationship with her as a game of tug-of-war, and you and she are both clinging to the rope for dear life, pulling. You can try strategies to get stronger and pull harder.

Or …

You can drop the rope and stop playing.

She cannot play tug-of-war on her own.

She needs you to respond in certain ways.

But you can change the script. You can act in a way that breaks the pattern and disconcerts her.

This is based on something I saw the British mentalist and illusionist Derren Brown speak of before. I've tried and cannot find a reference, but I do recall the essence of it. He suggested that a mugger, say, expects your response to be one of a limited number of options: fear, resistance, panic, freezing, etc. And so, even for a mugging there is an accepted script that both mugger and 'muggee' know and keep to. But what if you change the script? The mugger doesn't expect you to do something silly and unexpected such as breaking into song and dance. Derren Brown says that such an unexpected response will disconcert the mugger so much that he (the mugger) may well abandon the mugging. His (the mugger's) world-view has been shaken by your inappropriate reaction to the extent that he cannot cope with it.

So it struck me that the same thing could apply to narcissistic mothers, that if you respond in a different way it could put a halt to her narcissistic gallop. In a way it probably doesn't matter what that something different even is, once it nudges both you and her out of the pre-programmed script.

Now, this may or may not work. It depends on how vicious and vindictive she is. I often think the best way to deal with narcissists is to pander to them and give in to them until you can remove yourself. Often, there is no winning with narcissists and you're better not to even try. So proceed with caution with these ideas.

A lot also depends on your personal situation. If you're living at home or dependent on her, then it's probably best not to rock the boat. But if you're an independent woman with your own house and life, then you have more power.

So, for example, if she is whinging that you don't phone or visit often enough, your normal reaction might be to try to explain how busy you are with your children and job, or to itemise just how often you do visit, etc., to try to get her to understand and acknowledge that you do visit as often as you can.

But remember we spoke before about how narcissists are toddlers? And you don't reason with toddlers as they just don't get it. Same thing.

So maybe experiment with some different responses:

You could agree with her. 'You're right. I don't visit enough.'

This cheerful agreement, when she was expecting denial or remorse perhaps, will disconcert her. She may well snap, 'Well you should visit more then,' and you can then perhaps deflect with some whimsy, 'Hmmm, "enough" is an interesting word', you might say. 'Who gets to decide what is "enough", do you think? I think there's not enough time in the world, and it just gets shorter and shorter ...'.

You could try putting the problem back on her shoulders: 'Can you suggest how I find time to visit you more?' And then ask more questions about her solutions. So if her solution is that you give up some voluntary work, say, you could say, 'But how would those shelter dogs get walked and fed?' And if she says, 'Someone else could do it', you could ask, 'But how would we find someone else?' etc. ... Again, it doesn't really matter what you're saying, you're just deflecting.

You could try empathising with her. And this might be kind, because she probably genuinely does feel that you don't visit enough, I am sure. 'I know you'd love me to visit more. You probably feel quite neglected that I only visit three times a week', etc. Now, she might well accuse you of being patronising, but she might well soak it up.

You could be brusque and refuse to discuss it: 'Well this is how much it is, and that can't be changed.'

Or even be kind and refuse to discuss it, saying compassionately that this is how it is and can't be changed.

My point is that the programmed and endlessly rehearsed responses don't get us anywhere, and so it might well be worth trying something else.

In other words, drop the rope.

Hugs,

Danu

The narcissistic mother will never ever escape the Drama Triangle

Dear DONM …

We spoke of the Drama Triangle and how our narcissistic mothers are in it and have no desire to ever get out of it. And this is a powerful example of how they are stuck in life. As long as someone is a Victim, they can never improve their situation. And narcissistic mothers live their whole lives like this. They don't want to improve their situation because what would they have to whinge about then? How then would they get sympathy and attention? How then would they be able to blame those as they see as the Persecutors?

That would never work for them. And so, they remain resolutely on the Drama Triangle. And they try to get those close to them, such as us, their daughters, to stay on it with them in our allocated roles as both Persecutors and Rescuers, to allow them to play their role as Victim. They need this.

No wonder they protest so long and loudly when we move off the Triangle, when we refuse to play the part any more. If they are Victims, they need Persecutors of whom to be the Victims, and people to endlessly attempt to Rescue them from the fallout of their Victim-hood. And the Rescuers and Persecutors are often the very same people, including you. They don't want to be Rescued from being Victims of course. Just from some of the repercussions of it. And they don't want the Rescues to be too successful because what would they have to feel Victimised about then? But yet they want the Rescuers to try endlessly to Rescue them.

In this way I kind of feel sorry for narcissists. No, I never forget the damage they do, so my sympathy is very diluted by revulsion for them. But I can feel sorry for them too, stuck in their endless self-pity and need for approval and above all, their belief that everything they need is outside themselves. They have no inner resources at all. They are endlessly dependent on others to get what they need and want in the form of approval and attention and pity and whatever else it is.

So I do feel sorry for them. And in a way my pity empowers me and makes them feel smaller. And so I suggest to you that maybe you could think of them like this too. It's harder to be scared of someone you see as so weak and needy. And yes, they demonstrate that neediness in such a toxic way. But the root is their fear and weakness.

They're stuck in amber, fossilised, never able to grow or expand. They're stuck in their immaturity, their toddler selves. They will never know the joy of being what they need for themselves, of knowing they are enough *by* themselves and *for* themselves. I know the rest of us struggle with that too, but at least we can work towards it and know it's possible. They will never even do that.

Because they accept responsibility for nothing, to them it's a case that all circumstances are imposed upon them, and they're the victim.

It works, in some ways. It makes everyone else responsible for their well-being and happiness, and it gives them a stick with which to beat others if they're falling down on that responsibility.

But, no matter that they'll never realise it, living in victim-hood is not a wise decision. It is announcing to the world, and even more, to yourself, that you are helpless. And helpless is not a nice place to live. No wonder they are so unhappy. As much as they need this helplessness, I think they suffer from it too.

We are so much stronger and wiser than they.

Hugs,

Danu

Hurricanes and wind-bag mothers

Dear DONM …

I was living in London when it was hit by the 1986 hurricane. This was huge news because hurricanes are unheard of this side of the Atlantic. And I slept through it!

The first I knew was the next morning being woken by a frantic call from my mother: 'Are you okay?'

'Yes,' I said, wiping the sleep from my eyes. 'Why wouldn't I be?'

She explained about the hurricane and I told her I was fine. 'Don't worry,' I said.

She said piously, 'Mothers always worry. It goes with the territory.'

Even then that statement sounded false or 'off' to me but I couldn't figure out why.

Now, of course, I realise.

It's easy to say 'I worry'. It's easy to make a breathless excited phone call to sound concerned. It's easy to say the right words.

And it probably feels good, as a narcissistic mother, to do those things. She probably felt the glow of being a good mother, so concerned for her daughter that she phoned her straight away, always worried about her daughter's well-being. She no doubt felt excited at being involved, no matter how peripherally, in one of the biggest events of the decade.

And even better, it required absolutely no effort whatsoever. It didn't require that she listen fully, or put her daughter's needs above her own wants, or accept any wrongdoing, or be in any way less than her supremely selfish self.

And that is when I realised that a narcissistic mother can, and often does, talk a very good talk. But there is no substance behind it.

And that can be yet another confusing aspect for we DONMs. We feel the essence of the truth that there is no concern for our well-being, but we hear the words that speak of concern, and that causes cognitive dissonance for us.

But I think the truth is exactly as I have said: they talk a good talk, but there is only emptiness behind those words.

And I think our job is to 'listen' to actions rather than to words. The truth lies there.

Hugs,

Danu

Forgive yourself for your maladaptive behaviours

Dear DONM …

I think it's a fair bet that most of us have messed up big time in so many ways. I know I have. My life, objectively, is a huge mess in many, many ways.

Now, as you read the rest of this, know that although I speak of myself, that is only as a way of being an example. My life is part of the raw material I mine in order to decipher and make sense of being a DONM, and I share it here. But I hope you will read this and apply it to your own situation if it seems appropriate to you.

So, as I say, I have made a huge mess of my life so far. For sure, I have made huge changes for the better over the last few years but even so I'm still years behind where I should be. I'm doing things at 50 that I should have been doing at 20, and those missing years leave a huge gap which can never be bridged.

And, being fully honest, there are one or two issues that still remain to be resolved.

I know EFT works so well, and while I have used it lots and benefited lots from it, I don't use it as much as I should. And so I sabotage myself at many turns, both by continuing to do unhelpful behaviours, and then by not using EFT to help me avoid the sabotage.

And it's so easy to berate myself for the mess I've made of my life. I could nearly make a hobby of it in fact, beating myself up for all my failings and weaknesses and flaws. Itemising them like beads on a chain.

I'm all about personal responsibility. Our narcissistic mothers are the ones who blame everyone else for everything, as in: 'You made me do it!', and it's not a good trait. It's one I seek to avoid fully. It's very important to me that I own my own mistakes.

And, after all, I was the one who made the decisions I made. I was the one who put the first cigarette in my mouth, and so on.

But yet, I think it's reasonable to apportion reasonable blame where it's deserved. Narcissistic mothers kick us and then blame us for limping. And even more so: our narcissistic mothers kick us and then we blame ourselves for limping.

It is true that we are left emotionally and psychologically damaged by this awful upbringing. It's reasonable that we turn to whatever helps us cope with that, whatever we can do to fill the massive holes left in our psyche. It is fully understandable that we turn to addictions to comfort us and support us and be our friends when we can get comfort and support and friendship nowhere else.

And we don't know what we don't know. I honestly didn't know how to do life. And I didn't even know that I didn't know, so there was no way to even go looking for the information. I did see that others seemed to be doing life better than I was, but I thought that was because they were inherently better than I was. I thought my lack of life skills were my fault.

And too, my siblings who had the same upbringing as I did, seem to be doing better in life than I am. They managed to figure out what they didn't know, and get the needed information.

So where does the responsibility lie?

I don't have any categorical answer. I'm just trying to find my way through it all. I do think though that certainly I have blamed myself 100 per cent, but I think it's fair to say it is not 100 per cent my responsibility. My siblings achieved their successes *despite* their upbringing, not because of it, and that they managed to overcome it doesn't mean it's my fault for not managing that. And I think too that they're damaged in different ways than I am.

I think that we DONMs are very hard on ourselves, and we need to forgive ourselves more for whatever's going on for us. To hold ourselves appropriately accountable, but no more. And to strive to find where that point is.

As one DONM wrote to me (shared with permission): 'I am finally letting myself off the hook for some behaviour that in retrospect was appropriate for the wound I was carrying.'

And I am trying to do that myself, and I would like to

throw open that possibility to you too. Forgiving ourselves for our bad decisions doesn't mean giving up in any way. It means moving forward and striving from a place of self-kindness and self-nurture and self-support rather than self-blaming and self-loathing.

We did the best we could with what we had. We really did.

Hugs,

Danu

Finding healthy relationships

Dear DONM …

One thing that DONMs can struggle with is how to create and recognise healthy relationships. Many DONMs also have huge issues with trust which compounds this problem. How can we trust anyone at all, when we have been so fully betrayed by our own mothers? If she couldn't be dependable, how can anyone?

These issues make perfect sense given our background, the way we were raised with only unhealthy relationships.

And, in fairness, it's important to say that making friends and navigating relationships is a challenge for all humans, not just DONMs. It's part of the human condition really, as we are a herd animal, whose greatest survival skill is our co-operation, and as such we need other humans. But at the same time, we are individuals with our own needs and challenges and neuroses, and that's a powerful recipe for relationship challenges. So, as you struggle with this, don't for one minute think you are alone.

I Googled 'how to make friends' and there were over a billion – *a billion!* – search results. And Google estimates that 49,500 people search for 'how to make friends' per month.

So we DONMs are not alone in this quest, in this dilemma. How do we solve it though?

One solution is, of course, to give up on relationships entirely. And I can fully see how that is very enticing. There is huge safety in not risking relationships. We will never experience hurt or rejection or betrayal if we do that. But humans are wired to be social beings, and with few exceptions we do better when we have good relationships. It would be a sad and lonely life otherwise.

So, we need to learn consciously how to create and keep good relationships. (Yes, yet another thing we have to learn and do consciously when many others get to do it organically and intuitively. But not all people do, for sure.)

In the next few letters I'm going to explore those questions. Know that I'm still figuring this stuff out myself rather than having it all sorted. But this is what I've figured out so far.

The first step I think is to know that you're a good person, a person with whom people would want to spend time. It's not surprising that it can be hard to know that. Given the messages we got all our lives about how flawed we are, it can be hard to believe that.

As I said before, I recommend tapping (i.e. using EFT) the following affirmation: 'I am not who she said I was.' What I suggest is tapping on each point in turn (as per the instructions) using that statement 4 or 5 times a day for a month or two, and see the difference it'll make to your perception of yourself. Your narcissistic mother lied to you about who you are, and made you believe you were unlovable and unworthy and valueless. This simple affirmation, combined with the power of EFT, is designed to cancel out those lies.

The most important aspect of forming healthy relationships with others is to form a healthy relationship with yourself first. To value and respect and care for yourself. If you don't think you're worth those things, how can you expect others to think so? And they will pick up on your self-belief. In a way this is the goal of DONM recovery anyway, so it's just doing what we needed to do anyway.

The more you can be comfortable with being fully yourself, the better. That does involve risk, for sure, as there may well be people who do not like who you are. But others, I am sure, will be drawn to your authenticity. We can't please all the people all the time, and it's a total waste of time to try.

Another aspect is to enjoy your own company. Again, how can we expect others to do that if we don't? This does take a bit of a decision and a bit of determination, but it's so worth it. Not only are you more attractive to others, but you get to spend 100 per cent of your time with someone whose company you enjoy: yourself.

I went away by myself for three weeks last year, and I have to confess to being terrified by the prospect of doing it. Would I be lonely? How would I manage by myself? It was like diving in the deep end, not sure if I'd sink or swim. In the end I swam, gloriously. I read, I wrote, I dreamed, I explored. It was well worth doing and it mostly banished the fear of solitude. Not 100 per cent – I have to keep relearning that lesson and reminding myself that it's okay. But it was a huge help.

Paradoxically, the less you need other people, the easier it is to find relationships. People can smell neediness and can react to that. So the more you can be full and complete by yourself, and want relationships as an extra to an already full life, rather than needing them to complete you, the better.

So the more comfortable we can get holding that paradox, the better.

Hugs,

Danu

Meeting new people

Dear DONM …

First let's speak about how to find relationships in the first place. Often DONMs struggle with knowing how to make new friends. How do we approach people?

The trick is to put yourself in situations where you meet people. I think it's good to do something regular, as it's hard to make new friends from a one-time meeting. So clubs and volunteer groups are a good idea. www.meetup.com is a great tool for that, and local Facebook groups too.

Then – talk to people. Not with the aim of making friends, as that'll put too much pressure on you. Just for the sake of talking to them. (Obviously be socially appropriate about that.) Chat to people at the clubs and groups you go to, and people you meet during your day (again, as appropriate). Make it very low-pressure chat, just about the weather or something else casual. You may feel uncomfortable doing this, but it's a skill like any other, and so it'd be good to practise in low-pressure situations. Let yourself get it wrong as part of getting it right.

Show genuine interest in the people you're speaking to, but don't be afraid to share equivalent information about yourself, or it'll end up sounding like an interrogation. Also, a big part of talking to people is getting to know what you have in common. People like people who a) like them, and b) *are* like them. The things you have in common don't have to be earth-shaking, just common points of reference. So, for example, you might ask, 'Where do you work?' and when they answer you find some point of reference about that: 'Oh, I used to work just around the corner from there,' or whatever. You can then ask them do they know such-a-restaurant or such-a-person and take it from there. Do a Google search for 'making small talk' or 'making successful small talk' for more on this.

And then, as you talk to people regularly and see them regularly, you might find yourself drawn to one or two that you might like to be friends with. The first question to ask yourself is not so much about whether they'll like you, but whether you'll like them. Watch out for red flags – and we'll talk more about that – and pick well.

And then it's time to see if they like you enough to want to be friends outside the club/volunteer group, and so, when you're ready, it's good to take the next step and we talk about that next.

Hugs,

Danu

How to make friends

Dear DONM …

What do you do when you want to advance things from casual acquaintance, to see if someone would like to be friends?

When you're ready to take it to the next stage, I think the trick is to take a baby step towards them, and see how they respond.

Invite her for coffee maybe. Something light and easy like that. She will either respond positively or not. If she responds well, then great. Or another way I often take the first step towards someone is to invite them to a party I'm hosting, as that's very low pressure too.

If she's not interested and puts you off, either by a direct 'No thanks' or more casually than that (sometimes it's hard to say no to people, so they might just agree vaguely that 'Yeah, that'd be great sometime,' without following up on it) that's fine. It's important to respect others' boundaries by not pushing it. If I liked someone I might try once more by saying casually one day, 'We never got that coffee yet, must do that some time,' in a way that lets them pursue it if they were interested and just didn't get around to it, but in a way that puts no pressure on them if they're not interested. And if they still don't follow up on it, I don't do anything more. I stay friendly when we meet, but don't pursue it. Both for my own pride, frankly, and also for respect for their boundaries.

If they're not interested and reject your offer, then that's okay. In many ways finding friends is a numbers game. It's no reflection on you that they don't want to be friends. Not everyone clicks with everyone, after all. I know it's hard as it takes courage to do even that first baby step, and rejection is never nice. But the only way to guarantee never having rejection is to never try, and that can be a lonely place.

If someone makes the first move towards you, then of course it's easier. Make sure you really do want to accept the invitation though; don't feel obliged to go out with someone you don't particularly want to. It's okay for you to be the person who says no.

After the person has reciprocated the first baby step, you can make another step towards them, and wait for them to reciprocate that too. So, if coffee went well, you could suggest a trip to the cinema, or meeting for lunch. In a way it's like a dance as you and she are metaphorically moving towards each other. And all relationships should be reciprocal, so after you give one or two invitations I think it'd be good to let her offer the next one.

How far will the relationship progress? That remains to be seen as each baby step only brings you to that new place and at any time you, or they, can step back.

Each relationship is a kind of subtle negotiation as you are subconsciously asking: *What are we to be to each other?* Best friends? Moderately good friends? Good-but-casual pals, so that you just have fun together with no obligations or responsibilities? Mutual support system without being friends (e.g. two next door neighbours who take in each other's parcels and water each other's plants as needed)?

As these things are not usually discussed formally, it can be hard to know ahead of time how the relationship will work out, so baby steps will help the relationship find its own level.

There's no right or wrong about any of these different friendship levels, once each party keeps to the unspoken-but-very-real terms of the agreement, and both parties contribute and take equally within that dynamic. We speak more about equal contributions soon.

Also, as I said, in some ways making friends is a numbers game, so it's good to try to be as social as you feel comfortable being, so that there is no pressure about any one specific situation becoming a very close friendship. That'd be a lot of pressure for both you and them at a stage where neither of you knows yet how you'll get on. In a way this stage is very like dating where you are getting to know each other and see if you want to take it further.

And going forward we'll talk about deal-breakers and red flags, i.e. things to look out for, and after that we'll speak about the issue of trust, to help this process.

Hugs,

Danu

Deal-breakers and red flags

Dear DONM ...

I wanted to talk about both red flags and deal-breakers in relationships. To me the difference between these two is that a deal-breaker is something that only has to happen once and I am out of there. Red flags are behaviours that need looking at and analysing, and which *may* lead to me leaving the relationship depending on how things progress. They're behaviours that make me pause and consider and analyse. They are possible warnings.

I'm not very good at seeing red flags in the moment. I suppose like a lot of DONMs I was trained out of registering them or acknowledging them by all the gaslighting and invalidation. I have tried and *tried* to improve on this, but have not succeeded yet. It's as if my brain freezes during the experience, and I accept it unquestioningly. I am reliving my experiences with my mother of course when that happens. It's only afterwards that I find myself thinking: 'Hannnngggg on a second!!!!' as I revisit whatever the encounter was. I would rather notice these things in the moment so I can deal with them then and there, but as I say so far I haven't found a way to do that and at least I do notice them soon afterwards.

If you are the same, try to get into the habit of analysing encounters afterwards to check for any deal-breakers or red flags, in both your old and new relationships. You will have to do this consciously, given your upbringing.

Does it seem very cynical and calculating to consciously analyse your relationships? I think it's necessary for us DONMs, as I said. And you know, the words 'cynical' and 'calculating' have a lot of baggage and perhaps we could use better words such as *'careful'* and *'appropriate'* and *'necessary'*.

Perhaps we'll never become naturals at this and will always have to do it at least semi-consciously. In a way we're like someone learning a second language in adult life – no matter how fluent they become, they'll never have the accent quite right, and they'll never be 100 per cent comfortable. But they manage well and can communicate, just as we can learn to be alert for red flags until it becomes almost second nature.

These deal-breakers and flags apply to all kinds of relationships: friendships, romantic relationships, work relationships, and so on.

Also, a lot of these examples will indicate abuse, but not all of them. Others of them will just be situations that are merely dysfunctional through no fault of the person concerned; it's just that their relationship or life skills aren't up to being a good friend/lover/colleague.

These flags are also taking into account that there is no perfection, that even healthy people have flaws.

Also it might be interesting to look at each flag regarding your own behaviour. You might have some of them as a form of fleas. (Fleas are narcissistic behaviours that you manifest, picked up from your mother, without you being narcissistic yourself.)

In the following letter I list out my deal-breakers, and my flags in the letters following that. Of course, it's a spectrum and perhaps in the middle of the spectrum are behaviours that some would consider red flags and others would consider deal-breakers, so I invite you to define it for yourself.

Hugs,

Danu

What about deal-breakers?

Dear DONM …

Here are some absolute deal-breakers.

The first is if someone is violent to you. I honestly think there should be no second chances given for that. People who are violent can often apologise profusely and promise and swear they'll never do it again. So perhaps it's up to you if you want to give second chances for that. I would not, as I don't think I want to be with anyone who would turn to violence even once. But if you do, let the one chance be the only chance for sure. If they are violent twice, that is definitely your clue to remove yourself.

The second deal-breaker for me is if someone tried to control me. Of course, it's reasonable that they would hold me to appropriate standards of behaviour, but that's not what I'm talking about. I'm speaking about people trying to tell you what to wear, or how to style your hair, or telling you that you laugh too loudly, and so on.

Or, even worse, is if they try to isolate you from others. That's a favourite trick of abusive people, because if you're isolated you cannot get any support or any perspective different to theirs.

Now it can happen that a good person sees that someone else is bad for you, and wants to protect you. This can be especially so since we DONMs can be prone to having bad relationships already, so it's very possible that they are right when they say 'X isn't good for you.'

In this case, apply the deal-breaker tests, and the red flag tests (which we'll talk about next), to both people and see if you can find the truth of it.

One clue would be if the person is trying to separate you from one other person, or from everyone. Or, if they manage to come between you and one other person, they might then move onto someone else.

Certainly, if someone starts identifying *all* your friends as being bad, then it's a bad sign for sure. (Unless, by small chance, all your friends are bad. But there would have to be huge proof for me to accept that. I think it's far more likely that if someone is trying to separate you from everyone else in your life, it's they themselves who is the toxic person.)

Another deal-breaker for me is someone who doesn't respect boundaries. I *might* give someone a second chance on this if I think they're just being thoughtless rather than toxic, by telling them clearly, 'When I ask you not to do x, I need you to respect that.' But they definitely don't get third chances.

Also, watch how they treat people who are in a service situation to them; in other words, people they can get away with being rude to. Do they speak kindly and respectfully to them? Or do they take advantage of the power differential and speak dismissively, rudely or even abusively? To me that would be, and has been, an absolute deal-breaker rather than just a red flag.

Another deal-breaker for me is if they are a drama queen or king. I have written earlier about drama queens so I won't belabour it here, except to reiterate that it is definitely a huge red flag bordering on deal-breaker. If you get involved with a drama queen you'll be relegated to a supporting role in the soap opera that is her life rather than an equal partner in a healthy relationship.

These deal-breakers work for me, and give me a very clear sense of who I allow into my life and who I don't, and I hope that you will find value in them.

Next we'll talk about the less absolute and maybe less serious red-flags. We have discussed some of these behaviours before, but this is to have it all in one place, and to make it very clear that they are red flags to watch out for.

Hugs,

Danu

Red flags: Part I

Dear DONM …

Over the next few letters, I'm going to speak of red flags; in other words, behaviours which are not automatically deal-breakers but which absolutely bear analysing and considering.

In some ways red flags are tougher to deal with than the deal-breakers, as they're more subtle. But they're essential to consider as we DONMs can be prone to attracting more narcissists into our lives. It makes sense as we are primed for this kind of relationship, and so we need to be cautious and careful.

If I see these flags I don't automatically walk away. Instead, on the surface I continue just as I would if there were no flags. But I am gathering information, and I don't commit myself either in practical terms or emotionally until I can perceive the person better and decide for sure.

I have broken this information into three sections as it's long – there's a lot to discuss, and it's all important information.

And so to begin:

Be wary of people who try to get too friendly too quickly, and who want to be your best friend /soul-mate/lover too soon. Now, of course sometimes people just click. I have a friend of 12 years' standing who, the first time we were introduced, we fell into each other's arms like long lost friends, and it's a very happy and healthy friendship. So it absolutely can work.

But toxic people often try to seduce you (in the broadest sense of the word, not just sexually) very quickly, as they don't want to waste too much time or energy getting you into their web, so that is definitely a flag to watch out for. Don't feel pressured into responding – take things exactly at the speed you are comfortable with. That'll give you good information, because if they respect that, it's a good sign, but if they push regardless, that's a bad sign which shows they're willing to ignore your boundaries.

Similarly, be wary if someone is 'too perfect' for you, if you feel like they're your soul-mate, if they just *get* you and understand you like no one ever got you before. Again, this can happen totally naturally and genuinely, but it's also very likely that this is a narcissist or someone wanting to seduce you into their web.

It works like this: Remember I said that we like people who a) like us and b) *are* like us? Abusers can use this trait deliberately (albeit perhaps unconsciously). So they will be all over you expressing their admiration and respect for you, to make you think they like you.

And they'll do their best to make you think they *are* like you. So you'll be amazed at how much you have in common, from big things like life values, down to small details like their taste in music. If you hear them say, or find yourself saying very often, 'No! Seriously! That's my absolute favourite too!', that can be a flag. It might not be, let me stress that. It could be fully genuine. But my suggestion is that you proceed cautiously until you know.

I said a few weeks ago about sharing information with people when you want to be friendly with them, and that does apply, but balance is the key – don't share too much intimate or private information too quickly. Don't give any hostages to fortune that way. And be wary if they share too much private stuff too quickly with you. It could be just that they are over-sharers in an innocent way, or it could be that they're trying to quickly create an artificial intimacy.

Likewise, I am often wary of people who are extremely charismatic. Now, of course there's nothing wrong with people who are genuinely charismatic, and some lucky people just are. But also sociopaths and narcissists can cultivate a kind of manipulative charisma, and at first glance I don't know which category a newly met charismatic person falls into. Narcissists will give themselves away before long, for sure, because this charisma and interest is focussed on you, and they cannot manage that for very long.

Be wary of those who put you on a pedestal and declare you are just absolutely perfect, the most wonderful person they ever met, etc., etc. Narcissists can do that deliberately, the better to seduce you in what's called the *idealisation process*, and also because you'll fall even harder when they get to that stage of the game where they start criticising everything about you, which is called the *devaluation process*.

And people who suffer from Borderline Personality Disorder can genuinely think you are perfect as they are extreme black-and-white thinkers, thinking that someone is all good and perfect, until that person makes one mistake, and then becomes (in their mind) totally evil incarnate.

Regardless of why they're putting you on a pedestal, it's not a healthy dynamic at all. So anyone who praises you in superlatives is a bit suspect. It's nice if someone admires us, and indeed, if they don't find value in us, then why would they be with us? But excessive praise and adoration is definitely a red flag.

As we discussed before, if one friend doesn't like this new person, it could be that the original friend is the toxic one not wanting you to access someone healthy and good for you. Or the original friend could be right about the new person being bad for you. Judge this circumstance on its own merits, I suggest. But if a large percentage of your friends don't like that person, that's definitely a red flag.

Another flag is if anyone runs you down or demeans you. For sure they can disagree with you, and it's fair if they call you on inappropriate behaviour. But they should criticise your behaviour (if it's justified) and not your personality. In other words, they should comment on what you *do* rather than *who you are*. And any criticisms should be aimed at solving a problem rather than making you feel bad. For sure, even well-meaning people can have poor skills like this, so it's not an immediate deal-breaker, which leads me onto the next point.

They should be open to criticism themselves, once you do it calmly and fairly. So if they are criticising you in negative ways they should be willing to listen to you when you ask them to criticise you in healthier ways.

Hugs,

Danu

Red flags: Part II

Dear DONM ...

Here are some more flags for you to consider when you think of relationships both old and new:

In good relationships people should be willing to listen and honour your complaints. (Of course, it is your responsibility to make sure the complaints are both fair, and expressed calmly and kindly.) Someone who invalidates you or gaslights you or dismisses your complaints is not a healthy person to be around. We spoke before of how them listening to you doesn't automatically mean they agree with you, and that discussion might lead to compromise, or you seeing their point of view. But the discussion should be open and honest and respectful discussion in which your concerns are taken seriously.

They should operate a healthy friend-account balance, having deposited enough good things in the friend-account before they draw on it. And by that I mean, for example, that a new acquaintance should not be leaning on you for support when you and she have not built up that level of friendship. This is an aspect of becoming too intimate too quickly, but also of taking advantage of you. So long-term friends can certainly depend on you, perhaps even over months if needed, for example during a marriage break-up or health problem. But there will be a lot of friend-currency in the bank account already, in terms of times they listened to you, and babysat your children, and included you appropriately in their celebrations, etc.

Another red flag is if you feel exhausted and down and depleted after having been with them. In a healthy relationship you should feel good and energised and happy after being in the person's company. This is one for which there are exceptions – if a good and long-term friend, who has a good friend-account balance, is going through a tough time and leaning on you for that, you will probably feel tired and worn-out after being with her, and that's understandable and appropriate. But if you feel depleted after every encounter with someone, that's definitely a red flag.

There should be roughly a 50/50 share of relationship work. By which I mean they will ring or text you approximately half the time, seek out your company about half the time and so on. Conversation should be roughly 50/50 too. These things aren't an exact science and I'm not saying you should keep track and refuse to phone someone because you phoned last time. But if it's always you doing the work of managing the relationship, then that's something to look at.

They should be willing to do favours for you. Appropriate favours, of course. You wouldn't ask a new acquaintance to lend you a large sum of money or collect you from the airport in the middle of the night. But you can ask favours appropriate to the levels in your relationship-account. It can be a good way to test someone actually, to ask them to do you a favour. Narcissists and other toxic people will not like that, and their reaction will give you a lot of information. They might do the favour, but immediately extract a much bigger favour back from you. Or they might agree to it and then somehow 'forget'. Or they might wriggle out of it entirely. Now, no one *has* to do you any favours, and if someone decides not to, that's them setting a healthy boundary. But it also tells you the level of the relationship, and that's fine too. If they're refusing to do favours and yet wanting to know you better/be better friends/be lovers, etc., that is not right.

They should respect you. This means respecting your time, your feelings, your property, your autonomy and so on. If they are careless with those things it is a red flag.

Especially, they should always speak respectfully to you. Even as they disagree with you, they should speak respectfully. Even if they shout angrily or in frustration, they should do so respectfully. 'I am sooooooooooooooo fed up of you doing x,' is acceptable (of course, the less you can get to that level of argument the better). 'You're a stupid cow' is not.

Have they got any long-term relationships? It's a big red flag if they don't. Now, there can be good reasons for that –

DONMs can find that they have to clear house on relationships when they realise all their old ones were toxic, and that is no reflection on them (the DONMs) as people, for example. So it's not an automatic deal-breaker but it's definitely something to consider.

Along the same note, how do they speak of people from their past? There can be hurt and anger for sure. But is their tone vindictive and nasty? Do they accept any of the responsibility for what went wrong?

In general, do they own their mistakes and their flaws? Or is everything always the fault of someone or something else? This, you won't be surprised to hear, is a huge red flag if that's the case.

Hugs,

Danu

Red flags: Part III

Dear DONM …

One of my biggest flags is when people speak *at* me not *to* me. This is a subtle thing, but very real, and I bet you know what I mean. You can feel it even if you can't exactly pinpoint the difference. You are an audience, not a co-conversationalist. The speaker is engaged in a lecture rather than a conversation. They don't read any of your cues because they're not engaging with you at all.

I hate it when it happens. It feels so incredibly de-personalising, as if they are eroding my whole personhood and I am nothing to them but an audience. Now, I have no problem listening to people – I'm known as a good listener. I even have no problem with someone who talks a lot (as long as they'll listen in their turn when it's important too). But someone who talks *at* me is not someone I want or need in my life at all. It makes perfect sense really because of course to my narcissistic mother I was nothing but an audience. She (and my father too) spoke *at* me rather than to me. I have written before that I felt like a cardboard cut-out image of me, rather than my real Self, when I was with them. So yes, anyone else doing this to me is definitely a red flag.

Another flag is if they see you as flawed and try to fix you. There is nothing wrong with holding you to a reasonable standard of behaviour. But if it's a situation that they see you as a project in need of fixing and it's their job to do it, that's not a healthy dynamic. Honestly, if they see you as that flawed, they'll be better off without you and you'll definitely be better off without them. Being their project will be death to your self-esteem. It's also very toxic, as it means they will be controlling you and micro-managing and that's not good on all sorts of levels.

Likewise if they are someone you feel the need to fix, then it's not a good relationship. As we spoke about before regarding the Drama Triangle, you might be stuck in the role of Rescuer and that's not healthy for them or you. If they're that damaged, honestly, you need to walk away. You're probably not a therapist and even if you are, using those skills in personal relationships to fix someone isn't healthy. And as a DONM you most likely will have enough work sorting yourself out without trying to fix others. I know that fixing others is a good distraction from dealing with your own stuff (go on, ask me how I know – I have felt that pull for sure in my own life), but it's not healthy.

Sometimes we have to walk away from unhealthy relationships. But if someone uses that threat as a way to manipulate you, it's toxic. Again, there are shades of grey here. If you are drinking too much or abusing drugs, and a friend or partner gives you an ultimatum that you have to get sober/clean or they'll have to leave, I don't think that's manipulative. That's fair warning. That's trying to get you to realise how serious this is.

But if someone is constantly threatening to leave for all sorts of smaller reasons, as a way to manipulate and control you, that's a form of coercion and bullying and control, and it's not healthy. This is a very serious red flag and in fact, I would argue, a deal-breaker.

If you feel you have to hide your true self in their company, that's a flag too. Now, again, I have to qualify this. We all put masks on, and that is appropriate. One of the ways in which we grow closer to people is to drop some of the masks. But, in their company, do you feel like you are still you, just wearing a socially appropriate mask (which is fine), or do you feel you have to pretend to be not you (which is not fine)? It's subtle I know, but if you tune into your body and ask yourself the question you should be able to feel the answer.

So there you have it, a long list of flags to look out for. It might seem overwhelming to monitor all these red flags, but try not to let it feel like that. Like any skill, the more you practise it, the easier it'll become.

Hugs,

Danu

But who can you trust?

Dear DONM ...

DONMs often write to me that they struggle with trust issues. They might avoid friendships and other relationships because how can they possibly trust anyone when their primary relationships – such as the one with their mother – have been toxic and abusive? And like most DONMs they've been let down by other relationships too. No wonder they might want to avoid relationships altogether. And even if they don't avoid other relationships, how do they learn to relax with the relationships they have? They don't want to be tense and distrustful all the time.

I have thought a lot about this, especially since, of course, I deal with these issues myself. I recently had a very big betrayal by a long-term friend, someone I trusted completely, who let me down very badly. I am still reeling from that. How can I trust again when even she let me down?

So, here are my thoughts on this, and I hope they may be of some use to you.

I think there are three elements to this, and in a way it's about defining 'trust' differently. Or, allocating our trust differently, that might be a better way to put it.

The first is to trust in your discernment. We have spoken at length about deal-breakers and red flags, and how being conscious and aware of relationship dynamics can help you allow only healthy people into your inner circle. This means that you are automatically picking more trustworthy people and therefore it makes sense to trust them more.

The second way of looking at trust involves a kind of a paradox. Let me explain by speaking of something else first:

There is a paradox in how we live our daily lives. We consciously know that tragedy can strike at any time. Disaster can come out of the blue to change our lives irrevocably. The odds are pretty good that it won't happen, for sure. But the odds aren't zero.

However, we live our lives on the basis that those odds *are* zero. This is why people who have experienced disasters say, 'You never think it'll happen to you.' Or, 'Why me?' We have a belief that we are somehow shielded from disasters that can befall others.

I'm not criticising this, you understand. At a very deep level, it's a necessary psychological trick or we'd never function at all. If we allowed ourselves to truly acknowledge how precarious life is, we'd cower in our beds, never getting out, and then probably die of thrombosis.

In order to live any kind of a quality life, we have to take risks. For sure each person gets to decide for herself what risk/safety ratio she's comfortable with, which is as it should be. But I think no one takes zero risks. Everyone goes out into the street even though accidents can happen there. Everyone eats, even though choking to death is a very real risk.

And, here is another point: no matter how much we like to think we can live our life in safety, the fact is that we will die. Ultimately, we are absolutely not safe. This story only has one ending. But yet, we live as if we will not die. Again, we have to, for sanity's sake.

And so we live in a kind of half-aware paradox in which we know there is a good chance we are not safe today, and that there is zero chance we are safe indefinitely, but even so, we live as if that weren't so.

And I think this is the healthiest way to approach relationships. Yes, do your best to choose good relationships, just as you do your best to live a safe life by taking sensible precautions. And keep that kind of semi-alertness we do when we drive, where we aren't tense with fear and panic in every moment, but we are ready to snap to attention if a situation arises. As we drive, our subconscious is scanning our environment for us, ready to be alert if needed, but we don't have to consciously think of danger in every moment.

So I think the same thing can apply with relationships. If clues arise that something isn't right, don't ignore them, but at the same time don't fret otherwise. Trust that your relationship is good just as you trust your journey will be safe.

Know too that all relationships will end, just as all lives end, whether by death or break-up. I know it's hard to acknowledge, but this is the reality we live with. And so when a relationship ends, know that it's just part of the flow of life.

Hold your relationships lightly. Live as if the person definitely *won't* leave you, while knowing that they might. As I said, it's a paradox. Same as you know you'll be safe in your daily life and at the same time that you might not.

And then, the third aspect to trust is this: Trust in your own resilience. Trust that even if people do let you down, you'll be okay. We'll speak more of this next.

Hugs,

Danu

Building resilience

Dear DONM …

We mentioned in the last letter about trusting in your own resilience. I think this is an essential aspect to navigating in the world, with regard to relationships and everything else too.

And so I think a lot of the work we need to do day-to-day is in building resilience. It's something we need to build ahead of time so we have it when we need it.

Here are some thoughts on how to do this:

Self-care is important for this: eating well, exercising, enough fresh air, enough sleep and so on. It's hard to deal with problems when you're feeling under the weather.

Try to keep a sense of humour about life and its problems. I always try to remind myself that life is important but it doesn't have to be serious. There can be a kind of strength in dark humour. This is one of my strengths I believe and I can promise you it has saved me on more than one occasion. Humour really does help you cope if you can cultivate it.

Apart from finding the humour in your bad situation, try to take breaks from that situation by laughing in other ways. Watch comedies for example. Laughter is so very healing for us.

Another way to take breaks from the bad situation is to do things that require effort and/or concentration so that you cannot think of your issues – running, house-cleaning, painting, etc. –whatever you would like to do, that will just give you a break from the stress of it all.

As described before, in the section about how a cycling hint helped me, take baby steps to solve the problem.

Know that this too will pass. The pain will ease.

And, yet again, I remind you about EFT. EFT helps in times of crisis and upset to ease the emotions, to help you handle really tough things. I do find I can approach life with more confidence knowing I have this way of soothing myself and calming myself.

As we discussed before, another way (and this one is harder and for me is definitely a work in progress) is to become less attached to any specific person or circumstance. To work hard having my own happiness be a thing unto itself, not dependent on outside circumstances. To stop putting conditions on happiness, in other words. The only source of unhappiness is when reality is different from the way you want it to be. And there are two ways of solving that: to change reality so it's the way you want it to be, or change your wants so they align more with reality.

This isn't about giving up all desires or wants or wishes. A lot of the fun of life comes from identifying wants and desires, and going after them and I definitely have a very healthy wish list for circumstances I want in my life, both small and big.

But the trick is to want these, not to need them. To want them and strive for them in a kind of path *parallel* to your happiness, rather than a path *leading* to happiness in which you can't be happy until you get there.

More and more I'm convinced that this is the answer: to decide to be happy regardless. It's not easy though, and I am only attempting these myself. It's a new skill for me, and I keep failing, but I do keep trying, and yes, my happiness levels are exactly measured by how well I succeed in this.

And so I have come to realise that no matter what happens I'll be all right. I'll be okay in a way that cannot be defined, as there is nothing to say about it, as it has no conditions. I'll be okay because I decide that I'm okay regardless of circumstances. And that is resilience, and I do think it's probably the quality best worth trying to cultivate. The last few years have been beyond challenging for me, and this is the learning I have got out of them, and it was hard-won learning but it's so valuable.

Now, I'm not in some kind of enlightened state where I know this and live it all the time. I do get knocked out of it for sure. But I keep that knowledge (that I'll be all right) in sight, and come back to it as soon as I can after trauma or upset. And to the extent that we can do this, I think we have resilience, and I do so wish that for you.

Hugs,

Danu

Psychological abuse versus physical abuse

Dear DONM …

I have heard DONMs say, 'Well, at least she never hit me.'

I understand that, I really do. We are looking for any crumbs of relief we can get, any sense that it wasn't *that* bad.

But in a way when we do this, we are invalidating ourselves.

Because, the truth is that psychological and emotional abuse are in a very real sense far more damaging than physical abuse. And to the extent that physical abuse is damaging, a huge element of that damage is the emotional abuse behind it.

Physical injury is often not that traumatising at all. For sure, if you were involved in a car accident or such, you might well have PTSD from that. But ordinary injuries don't seem to cause psychological injuries. I myself was forever doing damage to myself as a child, having as I did a wonderful sense of adventure combined with a total lack of coordination or common sense. The road was trekked often to the children's hospital Accident and Emergency Department, to the extent that I am surprised it didn't raise suspicions. But genuinely, it was all down to me; there was no physical abuse in my house at all.

And those physical injuries have left no emotional or psychological scars at all.

And if someone else hurts you by accident, say they elbow you in the face by turning around quickly not realising you're behind them, once the shock and pain are over, it's fine. There's no issue between you and the other person about it.

So it's not the physical damage itself that's the problem.

If someone deliberately physically hurts you, it is the psychological trauma of knowing they are choosing to do this that is the real problem.

And if they tell you, and/or you believe, that you deserve this treatment, that you made them do it – well that is just another form of pure psychological abuse layered onto the physical abuse.

So, to summarise, even when there is physical abuse, it's really a form of psychological abuse, using force and injury as the method.

And, in ways pure psychological abuse, with no physical element, is even worse. This is for a number of reasons.

The first is that you don't even know it's going on. I describe this in *You're Not Crazy* when I discuss narcissistic abuse being a hidden abuse because we don't even know we are being abused. At least if you are being physically assaulted you know it's happening. Psychological abuse can be so subtle and subliminal that we don't even realise it's happening.

And because you don't know it's happening, it slips by your defences and goes straight to your subconscious to become part of your 'truth', i.e. what you believe about yourself. You don't get to analyse it or consider if it's true or not; you just absorb it wholesale, and come to think of yourself as stupid or unworthy or whatever horrible message they are giving you.

Also, even the worst physical abuse can only go on intermittently. Psychological abuse on the other hand can and often is pretty much constant. The undermining and snide comments and invalidation and gaslighting and so on – they can happen with the abuser's every breath nearly. And even if the abuser isn't there, we second guess ourselves so much it's like the echo of their abuse.

Another point is that part of the problem with physical abuse is that you don't know when the next attack will come, or what action of yours will set it off, so you are constantly on edge about that. But can you see that that is absolutely pure psychological abuse? So even though it seems to be about the physical abuse (and it is, of course, to a huge extent), it is also psychological torture.

So please do not dismiss what your narcissistic mother did to you, even if she's not violent.

Hugs,

Danu

This is not the life I ordered

Dear DONM …

One thing that I've been wrestling with about this whole DONM thing is how my life is not turning out how I wish. Obviously I have no parents in my life any more. I have a relationship with only one sibling, and that is strained enough. I have written before of how my marriage ended as part of this whole process. I am not really in contact with any extended family. There are other issues too, which are tough enough.

My life feels very meagre and thin to me, and I find it easy to lapse into feeling very sorry for myself about it.

Truly, this is not the life I ordered.

But this is the life I've got. And I can whinge about it and throw myself a pity party, and concentrate on all that I do not have. Or, I can embrace what I have and celebrate that, rather than concentrating on what I don't have.

There's an Irish proverb: 'You never miss the water till the well runs dry', which of course means that we take for granted all the good things until they're gone. I am trying to cultivate an attitude of celebrating the good things while I have them, even things we'd normally take for granted.

I remember as a teenager having a really bad throat infection, and literally every swallow was agony. I remember swearing that I'd never take a pain-free swallow for granted ever again. But of course I failed in that promise.

But now, when I try to celebrate the life I have, I think of that, and think of all the things I can do that others can't, things that are not to be taken for granted. All my physical health, for example, in which swallowing without pain is the least of it.

And, I've mentioned before how much I love cycling. I try to really really appreciate all I have that makes this possible: enough money to have bought a bike. Enough health to be able to cycle. Living in a place that allows me the cultural freedom to cycle. Living in a low-crime situation so that it is safe enough for me to cycle off by myself. Living in beautiful countryside that is a joy to cycle through. Living somewhere with clement enough weather that cycling is usually possible.

None of these things is a given, and I try to remind myself of how lucky I am to have them all come together to give me the joy that I experience from cycling.

And I try to expand these thoughts into all my life.

I fail often, of course. So this writing is as much to remind myself as to share with you. We teach what we need to learn, after all.

When I am tempted to sink into despair about the narrowness of my life, I realise it's only narrow by comparison in a specific direction. Yes, there are people who have far, far more than I do, in all aspects of life. But there are people who have far, far less, and I am so lucky and so privileged in so many ways.

I'm not proud of my self-pity, and often I think I need a good slapping, frankly, to fret over all I don't have and ignore all that I do. I get cross with myself when I start wallowing in self-pity and I do need to stop doing it.

I hope I don't come across as brusque or unfeeling. This is me thinking aloud about trying to find balance – to acknowledge and honour that things are not perfect for us DONMs without dismissing or invalidating that, on the one hand. But to acknowledge and celebrate what I do have on the other.

And hopefully to inspire you too, if and when you feel down about the whole DONM thing, to celebrate what you do have.

Hugs,

Danu

The road you're on will take you there

Dear DONM …

The Irish Tourist Board had a slogan a few years back, in pre-GPS days, which was: 'The road you're on will take you there.'

I do think it was them making a virtue of a necessity, frankly, in the sense of: 'It's a feature, not a bug!', because for some reason unknown to us lesser mortals, road signage in Ireland is dreadful. It's not so bad on the big roads, but on the myriad of small country roads it's inconsistent and unreliable. So it's very easy to get lost.

And of course, getting lost can be frustrating, even for an Irish person like me who is used to the system. I can only imagine tourists who come from more organised and efficient countries finding it even more frustrating and annoying. Hence the Irish Tourist Board trying heroically to frame it as a good thing rather than a problem.

Why am I telling you all this? Well, following on from what I wrote about it not being the life I ordered, I think that this motto, *The road you're on will take you there*, can be a good one for life.

Because the road we're on is reality. It's a fact. We can't suddenly magic ourselves to a better or different road, no more than we can magic ourselves back in time to make better decisions.

And so all we can do is to plot the route from where we are to where we want to go. And yes, we might be further away from our eventual destination than we would otherwise have been. But again, that's reality and all we can do is to go with it.

And, too, sometimes we have to redefine where the 'there' is that we're going. (Hope that makes sense!) I, and other DONMs I know, often mourn who we could have been and what we could have been doing if we had had better parenting. Depending on our age now, we might not ever make the 'there' that could have been possible.

The Irish Tourist Board was careful not to define where

251

'there' was. They didn't say, 'The road you're on now will get you to your original destination.' That would have been a foolish promise to make for sure.

But if we keep travelling, the road we're on will definitely get us to another place than we are now. And maybe that 'there' will be better than the other would have been. It will perhaps have its own joys and pleasures, unexpected ones, that we would never have got to experience if we didn't take this, the scenic route. The motorway is more efficient that's for sure, but the back roads are more interesting.

And even if this isn't true... Even if 'the road you're on will take you there', is just hype by the Irish Tourist Board's marketing team, and isn't true ... well, I think I prefer to believe it anyway. To live my life as if it's true.

Because I cannot change the road I'm on now. I can travel along it, and meet new roads, but I can't start from anywhere else than I am right now. And I would rather decide that this is a good road, than fret over the roads I've missed. I'd rather make the decision to be positive about it. And to travel on that road until I get to a 'there' I am happy about. And to enjoy the road I'm on now, enjoying its view and its unexpected gifts.

This is a decision I make. Sometimes I have to remake that decision, over and over. And so I do that too.

Hugs,

Danu

Last words

Dear DONM …

And so we come to the end of this part of our journey together. I hope you have found some value here to help you travel on in your journey as a DONM. In a way being a DONM is just an extreme version of the normal human condition: confused, making it up as we go along, compensating for our weaknesses, etc. It's a life-long journey for us all, and I wish you all the very best for your specific route.

If you'd like to keep in touch, please go to my website: www.daughtersofnarcissisticmothers.com

You can and sign up for my Guidebook there, and/or contact me. You might like to check out some of the various resources I have gathered to help DONMs too, such as EFT scripts for you to follow to make it easier to erase some of the issues discussed in this book. Find out more here:

http://www.daughtersofnarcissisticmothers.com/the-healing-store/

I invite you also to check out my first book *You're Not Crazy – It's Your Mother* as it's a good companion book to this one. It's like DONM 101. More details here:

http://www.daughtersofnarcissisticmothers.com/youre-not-crazy-book/

And, finally, I would very much appreciate if you could leave a review on Amazon for this book. It really does help me spread the word. Thank you in advance for that if it's possible for you.

Hugs,

Danu